# ART IN FOCUS
## Teacher's Resource Book

by
Gene A. Mittler

Bennett & McKnight
*a division of*
**Glencoe Publishing Company**

**Glencoe Publishing Company**
17337 Ventura Boulevard
Encino, CA 91316

ISBN 0-02-662270-X (Student Text)
**ISBN 0-02-667920-5 (Teacher's Resource Book)**

2  3  4  5   89  88  87  86

*Printed in the United States of America*

# Table of Contents

# Introduction

*Art in Focus* takes the position that *all* students can become actively involved with and profit from diverse experiences with art. It is not a text designed for use in classes with an *exclusive* studio focus limited to the preparation of future artists. It is true that studio experiences do represent a valued and valuable part of the content, but these studio experiences are combined with aesthetics and with experiences in art criticism and art history. Consequently, the book is designed to appeal to a wide range of students and not just the comparatively small number who have the ability and the desire to produce art. It is especially appropriate for use in a class where teacher efforts are directed at acquainting students with all aspects of art learning rather than involving them in in-depth learning in one aspect of art.

It is anticipated that opportunities for critical and historical inquiry will make studio activities more meaningful to students who have a desire to create their own art forms. In addition, studio activities can be extremely valuable to students who do not have a similar commitment to producing art. Indeed, opportunities to make art can contribute significantly to an understanding and an appreciation for art forms representing different artistic styles and incorporating a variety of media and techniques.

*Art in Focus* is intended to familiarize students with the many stimulating facets of art—with its history, its impact upon our culture, and the ways in which it is created. However, this is not the extent of the book's intent. It also seeks to prepare students to make their own personal decisions in art. It is no longer enough to assure students that Michelangelo, Rembrandt, Rubens, and other artists are great simply because society and art experts agree that they are great. Students must be provided with opportunities to determine for themselves the reasons for that greatness.

Personal decision-making is not restricted to encounters with the artworks produced by others, however. It is an important feature of the creative process as well, and students will discover this during efforts to produce their own art forms.

## Four Types of Art Learning

*Art in Focus* and the *Art in Focus Teacher's Resource Book* have been designed as a comprehensive art program aimed at promoting *learning of four kinds:*
- Learning to be aesthetically aware and sensitive to a broad range of visual forms.
- Learning from works of art, or art criticism.
- Learning about works of art, or art history.
- Learning to make art, or art studio.

The *Teacher's Resource Book* focuses especially on the fourth aspect, learning to make art, or art studio. The Studio Experiences contained in the *Teacher's Resource Book* are expansions of the Studio Experiences included in the text. These Studio Experiences are keyed to the aesthetics, criticism, and history aspects of the text. *These four kinds of art learning are regarded as equally important.* Nonetheless, some students may exhibit a preference for aesthetic, critical, or historical studies, while others may be more inclined to develop their knowledge and skills in studio. Although *every* student should be involved in *all four* learning experiences, there is no reason why those who wish cannot concentrate on the learning experience they find most stimulating. However, students should always be encouraged to share with others what they have learned as a consequence of experiences in aesthetics, criticism, history, or studio.

## The Scope and Sequence of Content in Aesthetics, Criticism, History, and Studio

The scope and sequence of content contained in *Art in Focus* and in the *Art in Focus Teacher's Resource Book*, constituting what is intended to be a complete and balanced art curriculum, is outlined on pages 6–7. An examination of this outline should indicate that the four major areas of concern—aesthetics, criticism, history, and studio—have been taken into account during the selection and organization of instructional content and learning activities. However, teachers should be aware that this outline is *not* complete, nor was it intended to be complete. New materials and approaches are expected to be added continually by teachers as they become familiar with this program and student responses to it. In this manner, the program can be effectively tailored to meet the interests, needs, and capabilities of diverse student groups.

## OUTLINE OF SCOPE AND SEQUENCE

This outline indicates the following:

1. What content is covered in *Art in Focus* and in the *Art in Focus Teacher's Resource Book*—comprising a complete, discipline-based program.
2. The location of learning activities designed to bring about student acquisition of this content.
3. Where the specific aspects of content are *emphasized* or *taken into consideration* in various chapters of the text and/or in the teacher's resource book. Dark-shaded squares are used on the outline to indicate where these aspects of content are emphasized. Light-shaded squares are used to indicate where these aspects are taken into consideration.

| ART CONTENT | LEARNING ACTIVITIES | | |
| --- | --- | --- | --- |
| | I. Learning to See (Chapters 1-3) | II. Seeing to Learn (Chapters 4-19 and Postscript) | III. Learning to Create--Creating to Learn (Teacher's Resource Book) |
| **I. AESTHETICS** STUDENTS EXHIBIT AN AWARENESS AND SENSITIVITY TO NATURAL AND MAN-MADE OBJECTS  Students examine a variety of objects from an aesthetic perspective | ■ | ■ | ▨ |
| Students recognize and respond to the literal qualities in artworks | ■ | ■ | ▨ |
| Students recognize and respond to the visual qualities in artworks | ■ | ■ | ■ |
| The Elements of Art: * Color (hue, intensity, and value) | ▨ | ■ | ■ |
| Line | ▨ | ■ | ■ |
| Shape and Form | ▨ | ■ | ■ |
| Space | ▨ | ■ | ■ |
| Texture | ▨ | ■ | ■ |
| Value (apart from color) | ▨ | ■ | ■ |
| The Principles of Art: * Balance | ▨ | ■ | ■ |
| Emphasis | ▨ | ■ | ■ |
| Gradation | ▨ | ■ | ■ |
| Harmony | ▨ | ■ | ■ |
| Movement and Rhythm | ▨ | ■ | ■ |
| Proportion | ▨ | ■ | ■ |
| Variety | ▨ | ■ | ■ |
| Students recognize and respond to the expressive qualities in artworks | ▨ | ■ | ▨ |
| **II. ART CRITICISM** STUDENTS DEMONSTRATE THEIR UNDERSTANDING AND APPRECIATION OF DIVERSE ARTWORKS THROUGH VISUAL DISCRIMINATION AND JUDGMENT  Students describe, analyze, and interpret artworks of the past and present | ■ | ■ | ▨ |

*'While learning activities concerning the elements and principles of art are emphasized in Parts II and III, a detailed introduction to the elements and principles is found in Chapter 2.

(Continued on next page)

| ART CONTENT | LEARNING ACTIVITIES | | |
| --- | --- | --- | --- |
| | I. Learning to See (Chapters 1-3) | II. Seeing to Learn (Chapters 4-19 and Postscript) | III. Learning to Create--Creating to Learn (Teacher's Resource Book) |
| Students make and substantiate with good reasons their personal judgments about works of the past and present (including their own artworks) | ▓ | ■ | ▓ |
| III. ART HISTORY STUDENTS GAIN A KNOWLEDGE OF SELF AND OTHERS THROUGH A STUDY OF ART CULTURE AND HERITAGE<br>Students increase their knowledge about artworks, the artists who created them, and the time and place in which they were created | ▓ | ■ | ▓ |
| Students recognize the importance of certain artists, artworks, and styles of art | ▓ | ■ | ▓ |
| IV. ART STUDIO STUDENTS EXHIBIT INVENTIVE AND IMAGINATIVE IDEAS IN THE ART-WORKS THEY PRODUCE WITH A VARIETY OF MEDIA AND TECHNIQUES<br>Students are provided with opportunities to work in the following studio areas:<br>Ceramics | | ■ | ■ |
| Design | | ■ | ■ |
| Drawing | | ■ | ■ |
| Painting | ■ | ■ | ■ |
| Printmaking | | ■ | ■ |
| Sculpture | | ■ | ■ |
| Crafts | ■ | ■ | ■ |
| Photography | | | ▓ |
| V. CAREERS IN ART STUDENTS ARE MADE AWARE OF THE MANY CAREER OPPORTUNITIES IN ART AND ART-RELATED FIELDS | | ■ | |
| VI. SAFETY IN ART STUDENTS ARE CAUTIONED TO EXERCISE CARE WHEN WORKING WITH CERTAIN ART MATERIALS AND TECHNIQUES | | ▓ | ■ |

■ EMPHASIZED

▓ CONSIDERED

## Organization of the Text: Part I, Learning to See

Teachers examining the textbook for the first time will quickly observe that it is divided into two parts. Part I consists of three chapters, the first of which acquaints students with a sequence of art-criticism* and art-history operations and indicates how these operations are to be used in subsequent chapters. Chapter 2 aims at impressing upon students the importance of a visual vocabulary. It introduces them to the elements and principles of art and underscores the importance of the elements and principles whether students are producing their own art forms or attempting to gain insights into the art forms produced by others.

It is imperative that students develop an art vocabulary which will enable them to understand and participate in class discussions pertaining to studio experiences as well as art-criticism and art-history experiences. Teachers should not only make certain that students learn this vocabulary, but should also provide them with frequent opportunities to use it. Toward this end, teachers may find it helpful to make extensive use of the Design Chart introduced in Chapter 2. Once students have learned the definitions for every element and principle on this Design Chart, they can make effective use of it when planning, creating, and critiquing their own art products. It can also be used as a guide when they attempt to determine how a particular artist has used the elements and principles to achieve a sense of unity in a painting or sculpture. For this reason, teachers might consider the advisability of having on hand full-page

*In this text, aesthetics is included in the art-criticism operations. Aesthetic theories are regarded as valuable guides to various qualities inherent in works of art. These qualities must be identified if those works are to be understood and appreciated.

copies of the Design Chart (Figure 1) which could be distributed as an aid to students engaged in studio or criticism activities. The Design Chart reproduced on page 119 of this *Teacher's Resource Book* may be duplicated for that purpose.

Of course, the art vocabulary can be applied during efforts to develop student sensitivity to natural as well as man-made objects. Teachers might well decide to ask their students to identify the various elements and principles of art perceived in natural objects. Many have discovered that this is often an excellent way of introducing or reviewing the art vocabulary. An appropriate time to do this would be early in the school year before initiating studio activities in which attention is to be directed to one or more elements or principles. For example, before introducing Lesson 3-2, "A Still Life with an Emphasis on Visual Qualities," the teacher might assign students to teams of two or three members and provide each team with a specific art element, principle, or combination of element and principle. A camera could be assigned to each group, or, if cameras were not available in the classroom, the teacher could make certain that at least one member of each group owned or had access to a camera. Then, as an out-of-class assignment, each team would be required to locate a specified number of natural objects that incorporate the prescribed element, principle, or element-principle combination. Photographs would provide a pictorial record of these discoveries, although students might also be asked to prepare a written or oral description. Later, the photographs would be exhibited in class, and students would be asked to determine which element, principle, or element-principle combination was illustrated in each. (This could easily be presented as a game-playing activity; see page 20.) As correct decisions are made, the photographs might be mounted

Figure 1.

## DESIGN CHART

| ELEMENTS OF ART | PRINCIPLES OF ART | | | | | | | |
|---|---|---|---|---|---|---|---|---|
| | | Balance | Emphasis | Harmony | Variety | Gradation | Movement/Rhythm | Proportion |
| | Color: Hue | | | | | | | |
| | Intensity | | | | | | | |
| | Value | | | | | | | |
| | Value (Non-Color) | | | | | | | |
| | Line | | | | | | | |
| | Texture | | | | | | | |
| | Shape/Form | | | | | | | |
| | Space | | | | | | | |

UNITY

in the appropriate sections of a large Design Chart (Figure 1) prepared earlier and displayed in the classroom. An effort should be made to mount the photograph that is most effective in terms of illustrating clearly an element, principle, or element-principle combination. These photographs, mounted on the Design Chart, would then effectively illustrate the various design relationships found in nature—design relationships which often serve to inspire artists.

Having themselves discovered examples of the elements and principles in nature, students would be better prepared to recognize and respond to the elements and principles found in works of art which spotlight natural objects. Students, individually or in teams, might be asked to vary the assignment described above by concentrating on the artworks reproduced in *Art in Focus* which include natural objects as subject matter. Thus, a small group of students could be assigned to identify artworks of natural objects which emphasize the element of color. Among the works they are likely to select would be John Constable's *The Haywain* (Figure 16.7). They should then be prepared to identify as precisely as possible the colors used in this painting, making certain to use the correct name when referring to each. This task will certainly require frequent references to the Color Diagram found on page 18 of *Art in Focus*. Another group of students, concerned with texture, might choose Hans Holbein's portrait of *George Gisze* (Figure 13.14). The members of this group would compile a careful inventory of the many different textures identified in this painting. No doubt, the teacher would ask these and other groups working on similar assignments involving the elements and principles to report their findings to the class. When these reports are made, continuous reference should be made to the specified artworks illustrated in the text.

Chapter 3 reintroduces the art-criticism and art-history operations, describes these operations in detail, and suggests a sequence for their use. More than mere academic exercises, these operations are employed during encounters with works of art, enabling students to acquire the knowledge and understanding needed for personal decision-making.

Teachers should note that both art history and art criticism make use of the same four stages, or steps —Description, Analysis, Interpretation, and Judgment. When used during art-history inquiries, these steps facilitate student efforts to gather information *about* works of art and the artists who created them. These same four steps constitute a search strategy when used during art-criticism activities, aiding students seeking to gain information *from* works of art. Thus, while the steps involved in both art-history and art-criticism operations are the same, they are used to gather different kinds of information.

Chapter 3 goes on to point out that art criticism requires that students know more than a search strategy. They must also know what to search for. For this reason, three broadly conceived theories on the nature of art are introduced as guides to various aesthetic qualities. Three theories were arrived at because no single theory of art was found to be satisfactory. There seemed to be elements of truth in several, and their degree of appropriateness depended upon the specific work of art under examination. Employing several theories of art seemed to be the most reasonable course to follow during efforts to isolate for study the aesthetic qualities inherent in a range of visual art forms.

While a considerable number of other theories were considered, the theories of imitationalism, formalism, and emotionalism were ultimately selected for several reasons. Imitationalism was chosen because it represents a point of view concerning works of art subscribed to by many students, particularly those with limited experiences in art. Most may not be aware that this point of view is indeed a theory of art. Nonetheless, they exhibit a decided inclination to respond with favor to works of art in terms of their literal, or representational, qualities. These are the same qualities stressed by the imitationalist theory. Why not then begin a consideration of aesthetic qualities with those that students already regard with favor? Teachers will recognize immediately the educational advantage to be gained whenever learning is initiated at a level with which students are already familiar and comfortable. After all, it is easier to move students in the direction of the unfamiliar if the starting point is at the familiar.

The importance attached to the student's knowledge and use of the elements and principles of art prompted the decision to use formalism as a guide to these visual qualities in art. The visual qualities, or elements and principles, are regarded here as the fundamental building blocks of visual expression. A knowledge of them is essential to students when producing or responding to art. The elements and principles represent a reservoir of potential design relationships from which student-artists select when seeking to transform beliefs, values, and feelings into visual form. And, students refer to these same elements and principles when attempting to identify the component parts of a visual composition and determine for themselves if these parts have been organized successfully to create a unified whole.

Teachers should be prepared to offer students ample opportunities to discover how a knowledge of the elements and principles can be instrumental to success when producing their own art forms and when responding intelligently to the art forms produced by others. Students must recognize that the elements and principles can be combined to form any number of design relationships and that personally conceived solutions to artistic problems require that they select wisely from among these design relationships. They must also learn to refer to their knowledge of design relationships during critical confrontations with the artworks created by others. Only then can they learn how those works were organized to achieve certain results. Teachers striving to promote learning of this kind pertaining to the elements and principles are urged to make frequent use of the Design Chart illustrated in Figure 1, page 8.

Having selected two theories that dealt with the more objective aspects of artworks, it seemed appropriate to include a third theory that concentrated on the subjective. Imitationalism focuses on the literal qualities, or subject matter, included in the work, while formalism is concerned with the visual qualities, or the selection and relationship of elements and principles. Emotionalism, however, directs attention to the ideas, moods, or feelings communicated to viewers by works of art. For this reason, emotionalism was selected for use as a guide to the expressive qualities.

Also contributing to the decision to use the theories of imitationalism, formalism, and emotionalism was the fact that these theories seemed especially well suited to the search strategy of Description, Analysis, Interpretation, and Judgment used when critiquing a work of art. During Description, students are asked to take an inventory of the literal qualities and the elements of art favored by imitationalism and formalism. Analysis requires those same students to determine how the principles of art also stressed by formalism have been used to organize the elements in a work. During Interpretation, students turn their attention to the expressive qualities endorsed by emotionalism to ascertain a work's mood or meaning. And, during Judgment, students take into account the literal, visual, and expressive qualities to render a decision about a work's success or lack of success.

## Organization of the Text: Part II, Seeing to Learn

The chapters comprising the second part of the text are designed to provide students with opportunities to develop, exercise, and refine their skills in critical and historical inquiry. To accomplish this, teachers are urged to involve their students in certain criticism and history activities *before* and *after* asking them to read any of these chapters.

## Activities to Be Carried Out before Chapters Are Read

Before reading any of the chapters in Part II of the text, students should be instructed to examine all the illustrations and then read carefully the captions to those labeled "Criticism." Responding to the questions included in these captions will enable them to gain information from the works illustrated. Moreover, they will be encouraged to use this information to make and support personal decisions about those works. As they gain experience in perceiving and responding to artworks in this manner, their perceptions should become more thorough and precise and their responses should be characterized by a greater understanding of and sensitivity to different aesthetic qualities. As a consequence, they will exhibit a growing inclination to discuss works of art and, as an important aspect of such discussions, to express their own ideas and feelings about those works.

For this reason, it is suggested that students be given opportunities to answer and discuss the questions in the criticism captions out loud while working with one or two other students. Sharing their perceptions, insights, and judgments will enable the students to learn from each other. In this way, they will also discover the need to develop and use a more descriptive, precise, and sensitive art vocabulary.

It would be well for teachers to point out to students early on that the captions do not include *every* possible question dealing with criticism. Ample leeway is provided for students to formulate their own questions as well, and teachers should encourage them to do this. As students gain experience and confidence in the use of the criticism operations, their questions should multiply and will tend to be more perceptive and sensitive. This will be a sign to the teacher that the students are beginning to see and think like critics.

The kind of critical activity described readies students for the information presented in each chapter. During this critical activity, students have examined all the works to be considered in the chapter and have been involved in critically responding to many of these. Their curiosity should now be aroused to a point where they will want to learn more about those works, the artists who created them, and the circumstances surrounding their creation. However, students should be asked to delay the reading that will satisfy their curiosity. This delay is called for to provide time for students to critically study one or more artworks in depth. This in-depth study requires that students describe, analyze, interpret, and judge a specific work or works in a deliberate and thorough manner.

As an aid to teachers, a listing, by chapters, of the artworks to be considered for in-depth study is included here.

## ARTWORKS FOR IN-DEPTH STUDY

(Continued on next page)

## ARTWORKS FOR IN-DEPTH STUDY (CONTINUED)

| Chapter | Title | Artist | Figure |
|---|---|---|---|
| 13 | The Entombment | Titian | 13.2 |
| | The Small Crucifixion | Grünewald | 13.9 |
| | Knight, Death, and the Devil | Dürer | 13.10 |
| | George Gisze | Holbein | 13.14 |
| 14 | San Carlo alle Quattro Fontane | Borromini | 14.2 |
| | David | Bernini | 14.5 |
| | The Conversion of St. Paul | Caravaggio | 14.6 |
| | An Artist in His Studio | Rembrandt | 14.13 |
| | The Eve of St. Nicholas | Steen | 14.14 |
| | Las Meninas (The Maids of Honor) | Velázquez | 14.20 |
| 15 | Embarkation for Cythera | Watteau | 15.2 |
| | The Swing | Fragonard | 15.3 |
| | The Attentive Nurse | Chardin | 15.5 |
| | The Third of May, 1808 | Goya | 15.11 |
| | The Giant | Goya | 15.12 |
| 16 | The Death of Marat | David | 16.1 |
| | The Lion Hunt | Delacroix | 16.6 |
| | Wivenhoe Park, Essex | Constable | 16.8 |
| | Haystack at Sunset near Giverny | Monet | 16.14 |
| | The Glass of Absinthe | Degas | 16.19 |
| | The Prodigal Son | Rodin | 16.23 |
| 17 | Pines and Rocks | Cézanne | 17.3 |
| | Starry Night | van Gogh | 17.7 |
| | Fatata te Miti | Gauguin | 17.9 |
| | The Fog Warning | Homer | 17.10 |
| | The Banjo Lesson | Tanner | 17.15 |
| 18 | The Red Studio | Matisse | 18.1 |
| | The Old King | Rouault | 18.3 |
| | Death and the Mother | Kollwitz | 18.5 |
| | The Scream | Munch | 18.7 |
| | Guernica | Picasso | 18.11 |
| | The Blind Man's Meal | Picasso | 18.12 |
| | Zapatistas | Orozco | 18.16 |
| 19 | Carnival of Harlequin | Miró | 19.1 |
| | No Passing | Sage | 19.5 |
| | Nighthawks | Hopper | 19.7 |
| | Welcome Home | Levine | 19.9 |
| | Swing Landscape | Davis | 19.10 |
| | Woman VI | de Kooning | 19.15 |
| | Sacrifice II | Lipchitz | 19.21 |
| | Humpty Dumpty | Noguchi | 19.26 |
| | Kaufmann House (Falling Water) | Wright | 19.30 |

Teachers may approach in-depth study assignments in a variety of ways. For example, individuals or small groups of students may volunteer or be assigned to prepare a critique of a specified work in a given chapter. Generally, small group presentations will be more effective than those made by individuals if teachers make certain that the students comprising the group are heterogeneous rather than homogeneous in their abilities and attitudes. Heterogeneous grouping assures a variety of perspectives and contributes to a more lively discussion.

The **Criticism Worksheet** (Figure 2, and in a format for duplication on page 120 of this *Resource Book*) is intended as an aid to students involved in these in-depth assignments. Teachers might require that students complete Criticism Worksheets as part of each in-depth assignment. However, it is advisable that teachers first caution students *not* to refer to information in the chapter when completing these worksheets. This is done to make certain that student critiques will be based upon information extracted from the works of art. It also increases the likelihood that student decisions regarding artworks will be their own.

It is important to dwell for a moment on the importance attached to student decision-making.

Without opportunities for personal involvement of this kind, it is unlikely that students will regard their classroom encounters with art as anything more than mere academic exercises. However, when students are free to make their own decisions about art and are encouraged by their teachers to express these decisions, the greater the likelihood that student interest and enthusiasm will grow.

Teachers may elect to have students complete Criticism Worksheets in class or ask them to do so as outside assignments. When they have been completed, worksheets may be turned in for evaluation or be referred to by students during oral presentations made in class. It is strongly suggested that the second of these alternatives be followed. Class presentations provide individual students or groups of students with opportunities to express their opinions about artworks and allow the remainder of the class to benefit from the presenters' in-depth studies.

Teachers should be prepared to hear a variety of divergent opinions pertaining to the artworks discussed in class. However, they should not be alarmed by this. In fact, differences of opinion are not only anticipated; they are welcomed. A consensus is *not* the objective of class discussions about art. Students should be expected to approach works of art with a range of different past experiences, and these past experiences will affect what the students perceive and will condition their responses. Class discussions provide students with valuable opportunities to express and defend their differing perceptions and responses —and learning is enhanced as a consequence of the spirited discussions that result.

It is advisable that students be made aware beforehand of the differences of opinion that are certain to surface. And they should be informed that these differences of opinion are, in large part, a justification for the discussions. Without them, discussions would be less lively and less informative. Examinations of any artworks profit greatly from a free exchange of ideas and opinions pertaining to those works.

Class discussions based upon in-depth studies of specified works of art need not be lengthy. Frequently these discussions will require no more than fifteen minutes, although teachers will find that student enthusiasm often causes the length to extend well beyond this. In any event, the value of class discussions, measured in terms of increased student interest in art, makes this time well spent.

### Activities to Be Carried Out after Chapters Are Read

The activities that students engage in *before* reading any chapter in Part II of the text encourage them to behave like art *critics*. The students assume the role of art *historians* when they become involved in the activities awaiting them *after* they have completed their reading of these same chapters.

In the first of these activities, students are asked to reexamine all of the illustrations and respond to the questions included in the captions labeled "History." Answering these questions constitutes a review of the material covered in each chapter. As with the criticism questions, it is recommended that students answer these history questions out loud while working with one or two other students.

Certain students are then requested to conduct in-depth historical studies of the same artworks selected earlier for critiques. It is suggested that the students who conducted the in-depth critical inquiries be asked to do these historical studies as well. Turning to books, periodicals, and other sources, these students should compile as much information as they can about the works of art, the artists who created them, and the time and place in which they were created. The **History Worksheet** (Figure 3, and in a format for duplication on page 121 of this *Resource Book*) should be used here as a guide for students engaged in these in-depth studies.

A word or two remain to be said with regard to the discussions generated by the in-depth studies, both critical and historical. Whether these studies are conducted by individuals or small groups, students should be afforded ample opportunity to share and discuss their feelings with others and, importantly, to use a precise and accurate art vocabulary when doing so. If this is done, there is a likelihood that the criticism discussions will be more rich and enriching and the history discussions more informed and informing.

### Additional Features of the Text

In addition to those already mentioned, *Art in Focus* contains a number of other features which will enhance learning. They include the following:

• A section at the beginning of each chapter entitled "Artists You Will Meet in This Chapter," which presents a few significant facts about each artist as well as a guide to pronunciation of the artists' names.

• "Enrichment" footnotes, which expand on items mentioned in the text and help to increase student understanding and awareness.

• "Criticism and History Experiences," suggested activities for each chapter included at the end of the book, which will further reinforce concepts and aid in review of each chapter.

• "Safety Notes," which give important information for safe use of art materials. (Additional safety information is included in the section entitled "Safety in the Art Studio," pages 110-111 in this *Teacher's Resource Book*.)

Figure 2.

## CRITICISM WORKSHEET

Name _____ Date _____

Title of Work _____ Medium _____

I. DESCRIPTION—DISCOVERING WHAT IS IN THE WORK (Emphasis: literal qualities stressed by imitationalism and elements of art stressed by formalism)

_____

_____

_____

II. ANALYSIS—DISCOVERING HOW THE WORK IS ORGANIZED (Emphasis: principles of art, which along with the art elements constitute the visual qualities stressed by formalism)

### DESIGN CHART

| | | PRINCIPLES OF ART | | | | | | | |
|---|---|---|---|---|---|---|---|---|---|
| | | Balance | Emphasis | Harmony | Variety | Gradation | Movement/ Rhythm | Proportion | |
| ELEMENTS OF ART | Color: Hue | | | | | | | | |
| | Intensity | | | | | | | | |
| | Value | | | | | | | | |
| | Value (Non-Color) | | | | | | | | UNITY |
| | Line | | | | | | | | |
| | Texture | | | | | | | | |
| | Shape/Form | | | | | | | | |
| | Space | | | | | | | | |

III. INTERPRETATION—DISCOVERING THE MEANING, MOOD, OR IDEA OF THE WORK (Emphasis: expressive qualities stressed by emotionalism)

_____

_____

_____

_____

IV. JUDGMENT—MAKING A DECISION ABOUT THE WORK'S SUCCESS OR LACK OF SUCCESS

_____

_____

_____

• A Glossary of important and/or unusual words, which are italicized and defined in the text. Many of the Glossary entries include references to text illustrations which are examples of the particular word defined. In this *Teacher's Resource Book*, all important vocabulary terms on each lesson-plan "RESPONSE/ PRODUCTION" chart are defined in the text Glossary. Other terms in the lesson plans which are included in the Glossary are accompanied by a note to that effect.

• A Time Line ("Chronology of Selected Periods, Styles, and Artists"), which will be of help in reviewing important artists and works with reference to their historical context.

**Figure 3.**

**HISTORY WORKSHEET**

Name _____ Date _____

Title of Work _____

  I. DESCRIPTION—DISCOVERING WHEN, WHERE, AND BY WHOM THE WORK WAS DONE

_____
_____
_____
_____

  II. ANALYSIS—DISCOVERING THE UNIQUE FEATURES OF THE WORK

_____
_____
_____
_____

  III. INTERPRETATION—DISCOVERING HOW THE ARTIST WAS INFLUENCED BY THE WORLD AROUND HIM/HER

_____
_____
_____
_____
_____
_____
_____

  IV. JUDGMENT—MAKING A DECISION ABOUT THE WORK'S IMPORTANCE IN THE HISTORY OF ART

_____
_____
_____
_____
_____

• Maps, which will help students locate cities and countries and visualize geographical features discussed in the text.

• "Art-Related Careers," an Appendix which covers careers in advertising art, graphic design, fashion design, interior design, industrial design, art education, museum science, arts administration, art therapy, and corporate art advising.

• "Books for Further Reading," which lists source books for each chapter of the text.

# Planning and Presenting Studio Experiences

"There is a vitality, a life-force, an energy, a quickening which is translated through you into action, and because there is only one of you in all time, this expression is unique. And if you block it, it will never exist through any other medium and be lost. The world will not have it."

Martha Graham

## Learning to Create—Creating to Learn

Growth through art is realized when students perceive, think, and feel in a way that reflects an expanding awareness and sensitivity toward the art forms they produce as well as those produced by others. This means that students must have opportunities to develop their knowledge, understanding, and skill in art through the production of their own art forms as well as through aesthetic encounters with a broad range of art forms that others have produced. *Art in Focus* is designed to prepare students for meaningful aesthetic encounters with artworks produced from prehistoric times to the present. The first part of this *Teacher's Resource Book* has been concerned with identifying criticism and history activities that will help students acquire the understanding and knowledge needed to make personal decisions about these artworks. The remainder of the *Teacher's Resource Book* is devoted to the detailed presentation of a series of studio lessons which will offer students opportunities to develop their skills in producing their own art forms. These same studio lessons are outlined for students in the text at the end of each chapter beginning with Chapter 3. They are designed to take into account the critical and historical concerns expressed in each of those chapters. However, these studio lessons do more than just amplify the critical and historical concerns of the text. They also enable students to express, with a variety of art media and techniques, their own ideas and feelings in visual form.

At least two studio lessons have been prepared to accompany each chapter of the text beginning with Chapter 3. It is highly recommended that teachers have students read each chapter and complete the criticism and history activities *before* embarking upon the studio lessons assigned to them. In this manner, students gain valuable critical and historical insights pertaining to artists, art objects, styles of art, and aesthetic qualities. These insights will serve them well when they engage in studio assignments in which they are asked to present their own ideas and feelings in visual form. Reading the chapters first introduces students to significant artists who can serve them well as models in the art studio.

There is an important reason for having students refer to artists as models in the art studio. Students are inclined to acquire information presented to them only to the degree that they find that information significant and relevant. When they discover that references to artists and their works can be of assistance during efforts to produce their own artworks, students tend to be more receptive to and retain more information about those artists and artworks. Therefore, by referring to artist/models in the art studio, teachers can more effectively augment student learning with regard to art criticism and art history while presenting models for student behavior in the production of art.

It is not expected that all teachers will find every studio lesson presented in this guide to be appropriate for their programs. Some lessons may contribute to particular program goals, while others may not. Some lessons may be too complex for students in some classes, too simple for those in others. These lessons are offered as examples of ways to link important criticism and history learning activities with equally important studio activities and thus provide students with a more complete education in and through art. In the hands of creative and sensitive teachers, they will most certainly be tailored to meet the interests, needs, and abilities of specific students.

## An Approach to Lesson Planning in the Art Studio

### Determining What Students Are to Learn from a Lesson

The studio lessons are intended to provide students with a foundation in drawing, painting, printmaking, sculpture, design, and crafts. Designing each of these lessons began with the formation of educational objectives. This was accomplished by first determining the information students were to acquire as a consequence of the lesson. This information fell into two major categories, one labeled "Response" and the other "Production."

The Response category included the following kinds of information:

| Artists or Art Objects | Period or Style | Theories of Art | Aesthetic Qualities |
|---|---|---|---|
| | | | |

The Production category included the following kinds of information:

| Subject Matter | Elements of Art | Principles of Art | Media | Techniques |
|---|---|---|---|---|
| | | | | |

When preparing to write educational objectives for a particular lesson, these categories were first examined and decisions made with regard to the categories that might apply. For example, if a lesson was intended, among other things, to provide students with information about Claude Monet and Pierre Auguste Renoir, the names of those painters were included in the Response category "Artists or Art Objects." If students were also expected to learn something about the art style exemplified by the paintings of these two artists, "Impressionism" was entered in the Response category "Period or Style."

Decisions concerning the Production information students are to acquire during a lesson were made in the same way. For example, it might have been decided that a particular studio experience should require students to use tempera to paint a landscape in which the painted surface was emphasized. It might further have been decided that the desired result would be achieved by using a variety of hues and contrasting textures. These decisions would be indicated in the appropriate Production categories. In this case, entries would be made in "Subject Matter" (landscape), "Elements of Art" (hue and texture [actual]), "Principles of Art" (variety and emphasis), "Media" (tempera), and "Techniques" (painting).

In Lesson 16–2 (page 90), Response and Production decisions identical to the ones described above were made. Even a rapid examination of this lesson plan reveals the information students are to acquire during this studio experience. This information is indicated with brief entries under the appropriate Response and Production categories. The manner in which this is done is also indicated in Figure 4.

| RESPONSE | | | | PRODUCTION | | | | |
|---|---|---|---|---|---|---|---|---|
| Artists or Art Objects | Period or Style | Theories of Art | Aesthetic Qualities | Subject Matter | Elements of Art | Principles of Art | Media | Techniques |
| Monet Renoir | Impression-ism | | | Land-scape | Hue Texture (Actual) | Variety Emphasis | Tempera Paint | Painting |

Figure 4. Information Students Are to Learn during Lesson 16-2.

## Writing Educational Objectives

As noted earlier, deciding upon the entries in the various Response and Production categories was a preliminary step in preparing the educational objectives for a lesson. There are two objectives for every lesson—Response and Production—and these correspond to the two kinds of information categories in each lesson. Response objectives are designed to help learners perceive and understand the art products of others, while Production objectives help these learners when they create their own art products. When writing Response objectives, care was taken to include every entry made in the four Response categories (Figure 4). In like manner, every entry placed in the five Production categories (Figure 4) was included in the Production objective. The Response and Production decisions made for Lesson 16–2 resulted in the formation of the following objectives:

A. RESPONSE:
   Students are able to correctly identify works of art done in the *Impressionist style* and can point out the main features of this style in paintings completed by *Monet* and *Renoir*.

B. PRODUCTION:
   Students complete *landscape paintings* characterized by a *variety* of *hues* applied as dabs and dashes of *tempera paint*. Richly *textured* surfaces are obtained by *painting* with short brushstrokes. These textured surfaces will contrast with the smooth surface of the posters on which the paintings are mounted. In this way, the textured surface will be *emphasized*.

Educational objectives like these provide a direction for the lesson and describe what learners will be doing when demonstrating their achievements. Teachers should note in particular that ample latitude is provided in the Production objectives for student decision-making leading to unique solutions to the studio problems posed. The opportunity for decision-making of this kind is essential if students are to become personally involved in the creative process. If additional opportunities for personal decision-making are desired, students could be permitted to make some of the choices concerning Production-category entries. This could be done if blank copies of the Response and Production categories (page 122) are distributed to students and used in the following manner:

• The teacher briefly explains each of the Response and Production categories and describes the kind of entries to be made in each.

• Several Response *and* Production entries are made by the teacher and discussed.

• Students are instructed to make a specified number of decisions on their own concerning the remaining *Production* categories.

• The teacher demonstrates how a Response objective is written which takes into account every entry made in the Response categories.

• Students are asked to write their own Production objectives. These objectives are to take into account the decisions they made regarding the Production categories as well as those made by the teacher.

• Students complete the lesson, referring frequently to the Response and Production objectives prepared as guides to learning.

• Completed studio products are exhibited and discussed. During this discussion, the works are evaluated in terms of how well they satisfied the specifications of the Production objective.

In situations of this kind, the extent of teacher influence is dependent upon the number of Production-category entries prescribed by the teacher. The more entries a teacher elects to make, the greater the teacher's influence. The degree of teacher influence is determined by the needs, capabilities, limitations, and interests of students. However, it is recommended that teachers specify at the outset of a lesson the minimum and maximum number of Production entries students are permitted to make. Otherwise, some students may attempt to deal with too much information in a single lesson. This could well lead to confusion and frustration.

Once students have gained experience and confidence in making Production-category decisions, they could be asked to make similar decisions concerning the Response categories. This would have to be done *after* a specific chapter had been read and criticism and history discussions completed. The procedure followed by students when making Response-category decisions would be similar to that followed for Production-category decisions.

One point remains to be made with regard to the Response and Production categories and individual student decision-making in this regard. To accommodate individual differences within a particular class, the teacher could specify several Response- and Production-category entries which *all* students *must* attend to. The teacher might then identify several other *optional* entries which could also be used by students who feel more comfortable working with specific instructions. These optional entries could be disregarded by other students who prefer to work unencumbered by detailed instructions.

## Making Students Aware of Educational Objectives

It is imperative that students know and understand the objectives for each lesson since the students are to be evaluated on the basis of how well they achieve those objectives. However, in the process of presenting a new lesson, teachers may not always remember to make clear, or students may misinterpret, the objectives of the lesson. The teacher might become concerned with the details of an impending demonstration, or students might be preoccupied with the prospect of working with a new medium or technique. One way of making certain that the major concerns of both the Response and Production objectives are enunciated is to present each student or small groups of students with a copy of the Response and Production categories with the pertinent entries listed, as in the example shown in Figure 4, page 17. Another approach is to prepare a large chart showing these Response and Production categories, which could be mounted as a fixture in the classroom. As each new lesson is introduced, entries pertaining to the different Response and Production categories could be introduced, discussed, and recorded on the chart. These entries could remain on display for the duration of the lesson as a way of keeping the students' attention focused upon the information they are to acquire. When the next lesson is initiated, the previous lesson's Response and Production entries are removed and a new set of entries recorded.

## Lesson-Plan Visuals

The visuals used in each lesson reflect the decisions made regarding the Response and Production categories. Once these decisions were made, attention was directed to identifying the artists and works of art that best exemplified the Response and Production concerns. In Lesson 16–2, for example, paintings done by Claude Monet and Pierre Auguste Renoir in the style of Impressionism are listed on the lesson plan under "Visuals." The choice of these paintings was based upon the decisions made earlier regarding the Response categories "Artists or Art Objects" and "Period or Style." All visuals specified in the lesson plans included in this *Teacher's Resource Book* are found in the *Art in Focus* text.*

## Materials and Tools Needed for the Lessons

The materials and tools needed for each lesson are specified, although teachers will readily recognize instances where substitutions can be made. Many of

---

*The only exception is found in Lesson 5–3, where reference is made to Egyptian sarcophagi covers. While no such sarcophagi covers are illustrated in the text, teachers should have little difficulty finding examples in books dealing specifically with Egyptian art.

the painting experiences, for example, can be done with acrylic rather than tempera paint. Tempera paint was specified in most painting lessons simply because this medium is less expensive and, consequently, more likely to be found in most classrooms.

An effort was made to expose students to a range of media and techniques. However, teachers are certain to note some unintentioned omissions, which they may choose to rectify. When doing so, it is suggested that they follow the approach to lesson planning described in this *Teacher's Resource Book*. Considerable importance is attached to the use of the Response and Production categories as a way of preparing clear objectives and selecting explicit content. Attending to these categories when designing a lesson enables teachers to clarify in their own minds what they expect students to learn and facilitates the formation of specific educational objectives.

## Presentation of the Lessons

Each lesson plan includes an outline describing the steps involved in presenting the lesson to learners. Teachers will want to familiarize themselves with this portion of the lesson plan before introducing any lesson. During an initial reading, they should consider the *instructional strategy or strategies* which might be used most effectively to stimulate and maintain student interest and involvement.

Instructional strategies are defined here as the different ways in which teachers conduct classroom instruction and interaction. When deciding upon an instructional strategy to be used in a given situation, teachers are advised to base their choice upon whether or not they are comfortable with it and if they feel it is the most effective strategy to use in that situation. More often than not their choice will be made from the following list of instructional strategies:

- Lecture.
- Discussion.
- Game playing.
- Demonstration.
- Individual problem-solving.
- Group problem-solving.

A lesson's success is frequently dependent upon the instructional strategy selected and the skill with which that instructional strategy is applied. This more than justifies a closer look at each type of strategy.

### Lecture

The advantage of the lecture method is that it offers teachers the opportunity to communicate economically with a large audience. It is most often employed in situations where teachers face the task of presenting students with a great deal of information in a short period of time. With a lecture, teachers can personally present the major points of a lesson, use their own interest and enthusiasm to inspire students, and tailor their presentations in keeping with student responses. But, claims for expediency notwithstanding, the lecture method is somewhat tarnished when one considers its effectiveness.

All too often the lecture method fails to sustain student attention or participation. Students tend to become passive participants in the learning process as attention directed to the lecturer wavers. There is reason to believe that students retain less than twenty percent of the information received by way of a lecture. This is ample justification to use the lecture with discretion, particularly in the art studio where more visual means of communication are more appropriate.

## Discussion

Stimulating students to become actively involved in discussions about their artwork or the artwork of others is, as every teacher knows, an effective way of sparking and sustaining student interest and enthusiasm. Usually, the teacher acts as the moderator-leader and guides the communicative interaction to conform to the instructional objectives of a lesson. Discussions allow learners to express themselves and to interact with each other. As a consequence, *they learn from each other*. The satisfaction generated by discussion sessions serves to prepare students for subsequent learning experiences, enhances learning outcomes, contributes to class morale, and prompts students to identify what they know and do not know.

However, teachers should be sensitive to the limitations of the discussion method and work to overcome those limitations. Although discussions are intended to promote student thinking and participation, they can easily evolve into lecture-type situations. Teachers must be on guard not to dominate discussions or rely on "fact" questions that leave no room for personal opinion and can be answered with a single word, a brief phrase, or even a simple "yes" or "no." When responding to fact questions, students are in effect talking to the teacher rather than to each other. And their responses are frequently predicated upon a desire to "give the teacher what he or she wants to hear."

Another limitation of the discussion method is that not all students are self-confident enough to participate. A discussion may in fact involve only a handful of self-reliant, assertive students, with the remainder of the class assuming roles as passive onlookers. A discussion can only be effective if all class members take part. It is the teacher's responsibility to make every effort to entice as many students as possible to participate in class discussions. But this is not always as easy as it sounds. One possible route to success in this regard involves building student self-confidence. The small group discussions pertaining to questions found in the captions for text illustrations may be one way of initiating this self-confidence. And, it might be nurtured as students present and discuss information gained from in-depth criticism and history inquiries regarding specific works of art and the artists who created them.

As a further aid to effective discussions, teachers may want to point out to students that they should listen to what others have to say, take turns speaking, and plan ahead what they themselves will say. Teachers may also want to arrange seating assignments so that students can make eye contact and can hear clearly each other's remarks.

## Game Playing

A third instructional strategy is game playing, an approach that represents a stimulating change of pace from the more common information-dispensing methods of instruction.

In a game-playing activity, students may be asked to design personal solutions to problems posed in the context of artificially produced situations. They become *players,* rather than spectators, in the learning process. In some cases, they are provided with certain clues and are asked to perform as if the situation in which they have been asked to place themselves is real. For example, students may be asked to project themselves back in time to the Medieval period. There, they find themselves in the service of a powerful king. The king has just heard from a passing knight about the attributes of a new gastronomic novelty known as a "sandwich." His curiosity aroused, the king decides that he must sample one of these sandwiches for himself. He summons together the members of his court and commands each to design a sandwich for him. The most appealing of these will be prepared by the royal chef and served to the king. Knowing little about sandwiches or their appearance, the king's only specifications are based upon the few clues offered by the passing knight. As a result, he commands that the sandwiches must include two slices of bread and no less than six different ingredients. Students, acting as members of the king's court, are thus to design a "sandwich fit for a king" —utilizing materials and techniques specified by the teacher. In their assigned roles, students are to be as ignorant of a sandwich's appearance as is the king. Consequently, they are at liberty to be as whimsical and creative in their designs as their imaginations allow them to be. (See Figures 5 and 6 for examples of student sandwich designs completed in this game-playing manner.)

Another example of the game-playing strategy is found in Lesson 5–2. In this lesson, students are first asked to imagine themselves living in the culture of the ancient Egyptians. The students are then asked to

Figure 6. Sandwich design created as a result of game-playing strategy.

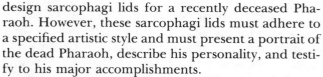

Figure 5. Sandwich design created as a result of game-playing strategy.

design sarcophagi lids for a recently deceased Pharaoh. However, these sarcophagi lids must adhere to a specified artistic style and must present a portrait of the dead Pharaoh, describe his personality, and testify to his major accomplishments.

Different game-playing approaches will be found in several other lessons outlined in this resource book. For teachers who have used game playing in the art studio before, these lessons may suggest some new directions. For those who have never attempted this approach, these lessons will serve as an introduction to an exciting and effective method of instruction.

### Demonstration

The instructional strategy that is probably the most familiar to art teachers is demonstration. Rarely does the art teacher introduce a new medium or a new technique without demonstrating how that medium or technique can and should be used. As they examine the lessons in this resource book, teachers will recognize many situations where demonstrations are called for. Teachers are encouraged to use this instructional strategy whenever possible since it is an especially effective method of instruction when applied to studio activities.

New teachers are advised never to enter into a class demonstration without practicing beforehand *with the same materials students will be expected to use*. Considerable embarrassment can be avoided and credibility preserved if teachers are able to tell and then show students exactly what to expect when a particular medium is used in a certain way. The time to discover that the black ink in the unmarked jar is *not* India ink is beforehand—not when trying unsuccessfully to wash it off a painted surface during a paper batik demonstration before the entire class (Lesson 17–2). Practicing in advance also enables the teacher to anticipate the questions that are certain to arise, especially during more involved lessons.

Of course, it is important to make certain that every student has a good view of the demonstration. And, as with any instructional strategy, teachers should expect students to be quiet and attentive before beginning. It is wise to hold firmly to the promise not to begin until they are. Finally, teachers are urged to include continuous commentary with their demonstrations. They should not assume that students can understand what is going on by watching a demonstration carried out in silence or near silence. Teachers should develop the habit of explaining in detail what they are doing and why they are doing it *as they demonstrate*. To be of maximum value to students, the demonstration must be amplified by a detailed explanation of every action. When this is done, students receive information by way of the eyes *and* ears, increasing the likelihood that this information will be understood and assimilated.

### Individual Problem-Solving

Teachers are in effect employing another instructional strategy when they pose studio problems and ask students to engage in personal decision-making while searching for unique solutions to those problems. However, this instructional strategy requires a classroom climate that encourages students to become actively involved in seeking, discovering, and selecting from a range of possible answers rather than asking them to converge on predetermined "right answers." A climate that generates problem-solving activity in the art studio requires teachers who are more concerned with opening the learner's mind than with merely filling it.

Problem-solving in art involves the learner in a number of important steps. The teacher must be conscious of these steps and be prepared to lend support and encouragement to students at each of them. These steps consist of the following:
- Recognizing the problem.
- Clarifying the problem.
- Formulating alternative solutions.
- Evaluating the alternative solutions.
- Selecting the most promising solution, refining it, and putting it into practice.
- Assessing the effectiveness of the solution.

It is the teacher's responsibility to present and clarify the problem. Clarification involves making students aware of the parameters and the major concerns of the problem. These include the specific subject matter, elements of art, principles of art, media, and techniques that students are to attend to when formulating alternative solutions.*

As noted earlier, the teacher sets the stage for problem-solving by fostering a classroom climate that offers students the freedom to pursue, within specified boundaries, independent solutions and engage in learning that is increasingly self-directed. This means that teachers must prepare and present educational objectives that designate clearly the parameters

---

*Teachers will observe that these concerns are accommodated in the Production categories discussed earlier and illustrated in Figure 4, page 17.

of each artistic problem. They must also be prepared to encourage, value, and respect the highly personal solutions arrived at by students working within these parameters.

During the final evaluative stage of problem-solving, teachers provide students with in-class opportunities for critiques. At this time, the parameters of the problem are reviewed and students are able to diagnose for themselves the effectiveness of their solutions. Critiques are such an indispensable and important aspect of learning in the art studio that additional comments pertaining to them will be offered in a subsequent section of this *Teacher's Resource Book* (page 23).

The student problem-solving behavior outlined above reflects, albeit at a more rudimentary level, the problem-solving behavior of artists. It is appropriate that students working in an art class learn to know and do what artists know and do. But students can be expected to exhibit behavior of this kind only when they, like artists, have the freedom to make personal choices when confronting artistic problems. Only then can they experience the frustrations, the disappointments, and the joys that are a part of the creative effort—and make that effort exciting and rewarding.

It is important that students be provided with more than mere exposure to art concepts, techniques, and materials. They must also be encouraged to utilize these concepts, techniques, and materials to fashion art products that reflect *their* ideas, beliefs, and feelings. The studio lessons provided in this resource book attempt to do this.

However, these lessons, or any other lessons for that matter, cannot be expected to achieve worthwhile learning outcomes unless teachers present them in an exciting and imaginative manner. Creative and enthusiastic teachers can expect to have creative and enthusiastic students. In the final analysis, it is not the content so much as teacher effectiveness that determines the level of learning that takes place in the classroom.

### Group Problem-Solving

Group problem-solving, in which small groups of students are asked to work together to solve studio problems posed by the teacher, can also be regarded as an instructional method. The educational advantage offered by this approach is that it provides for a good deal of give-and-take between group members. Students can express their ideas and interact with each other as they engage in a cooperative effort to solve an artistic problem.

Problem-solving activities presented in small group settings can often be helpful for students who have had difficulties arriving at solutions when working alone. Group activities enable them to learn from others while building their own self-confidence. For this reason, it is important that teachers do not randomly assign students to groups. Inadvertently assigning students with leadership qualities to the same group could well result in tension, conflict, and hostility. On the other hand, a group composed of students accustomed to following the lead of others is likely to exhibit little if any progress toward the solution of a problem. Effective grouping requires a conscientious effort on the part of the teacher to include leaders and followers in each group.

## Evaluation of the Lesson

The most important concern of teachers and students as the lessons in this resource book are completed should be determining *what was learned* from each lesson. This learning will be exemplified in the students' response and in the art products the students create as they devise their own solutions to the studio problems. Evaluation is conducted to ascertain if the knowledge, understanding, and skills specified in the Response and Production objectives have been acquired. Teachers can accomplish this by observing student behavior both in studio work and in responses made during and immediately after each learning episode. For example, evidence that students have gained an understanding of how to create a variety of actual textures (Lesson 10–3) would be found in artworks that make effective use of this combination of element (texture) and principle (variety).

Teacher efforts at evaluation often involve the preparation of questions derived from and directly related to lesson objectives. Such an approach has been adopted in the evaluation section prepared for each lesson in this resource book. Answers to evaluation questions provide the data teachers use when determining the effectiveness of their teaching and the extent of student learning. Answers are based upon observations of (1) student responses made during discussions of their own artworks as well as artworks produced by others and (2) student solutions to studio problems.

## Student Critiques

It was suggested earlier that the Criticism Worksheet (Figure 2, page 14) can be an aid to students during in-depth examinations of artworks. Its usefulness need not end there, however. This worksheet can also be used while students are actively engaged in creating their own artworks and when they attempt to determine the level of success achieved by those artworks. Completing the worksheet while they are creating works of art helps students clarify in their own minds what they hope to do and how they might best go about doing it. Moreover, sharing decisions indicated on the worksheet with the teacher is helpful to both the student and the teacher. The student is able to communicate more clearly his or her intentions to the teacher. And, as a consequence, the teacher is in a better position to offer more pertinent and specific suggestions. Once students have completed their artworks, the Criticism Worksheet can be used to stimulate in-depth critiques of those works.

Too often class critiques fail to generate enthusiasm and active participation on the part of students. When they do volunteer an observation with regard to a work they produced or one produced by someone else, the observation tends to be vague and uncertain. For this reason, the teacher frequently finds it necessary to assume a major role in the critique, while students act as mere receivers of information. The Criticism Worksheet can help rectify this. Once students have become familiar with it, the worksheet can be used to direct their attention to the aesthetic qualities in the works being critiqued. In other words, it helps them identify what to look for and what to respond to. Given time to complete worksheets before a critique, students can be expected to make comments pertaining to what is portrayed in a work (Description), how effectively the work is organized (Analysis), what ideas or feelings are communicated (Interpretation), and whether or not they feel the work is a successful resolution of the artistic problem (Judgment). The teacher's task is to guide the critique by posing questions pertaining to each of these critical operations.

One final comment is needed with regard to critiques, both critiques of the students' own artworks and those directed at works produced by others. If actual artworks, prints, or slides are used, students wishing to make comments about some feature or quality observed in a work should be asked to leave their desks or tables, go to the work, and point out that feature or quality. It is not recommended that they remain in their seats when offering their observations and opinions. Rather, they should become physically as well as mentally involved to the extent that they move up to the work and, with hands and fingers, clearly indicate to what they are referring.

## Instruction for Students with Special Needs

Learning in the art classroom, whether it be related to art history, art criticism, or studio art, can be a meaningful and rewarding experience for students with special needs. They may include the emotionally disturbed, the mentally retarded, or the physically handicapped. Much depends upon the teacher's ability to adjust instructional methods so as to provide the best learning environment for such students. Of prime importance is the need to take special care at the outset of the class to welcome the special student and to make him or her feel comfortable within the class situation.

Once classroom work is underway, there are a number of steps the teacher can take to help the special student gain as much as possible from the class. The following points and strategies should be helpful with regard to using *Art in Focus* in classes of which students with special needs are a part, though care should be taken to adjust any strategy to a student's *individual* needs.

• Teachers should have students work in teams, with one special student to a team. In this way, the special student can benefit from watching others as they complete their work and can learn from the other students' explanations of the work in progress.

• Special students should be allowed to progress at their own rate in completing class work.

• Many special education students find greater success if work assignments and instructions are broken up into small segments. This makes it easier for them to complete a task and, thus, gain confidence in their abilities.

• The teacher should also be ready to repeat instructions whenever necessary to insure that the assignment has been understood. These repeated directions should be stated in different ways each time, from different points of view, leading to greater chances for understanding.

• The teacher should also try to be as visual as possible. This means using as many visual aids as time and resources will allow. Students with special needs will benefit by receiving information by way of the eyes, as well as the ears.

• With special students, demonstrations by the teacher become even more important. Most students enjoy—and learn much from—seeing what is being done. For this reason, it is necessary to make sure that they have good seats at the front of the class so that demonstrations can be seen easily.

• It is also helpful for the teacher to simplify instructions. This makes it easier for instructions to be understood and tasks to be completed, thus building confidence. After each demonstration, the teacher will need to go to special students first to make sure that they have no questions as they begin working. Such students may become frustrated if they see the other students doing a task well and find that they themselves are having difficulty.

• Any of the subject areas of *Art in Focus* are appropriate for the special student. Of the steps of Description, Analysis, Interpretation, and Judgment, the easiest for most will be Description. Most will have no trouble identifying what they see in a work of art. Judgments of works, even negative ones, should be encouraged, since there are no right or wrong answers. Once the students find that even their negative reactions are accepted, they may become confident enough to venture other, more informed views. The teacher should look for special students to raise their hands in discussions of Analysis and Interpretation as well, and should call on them whenever possible.

• The visually impaired student will benefit from the tactile sensations which claywork, collage, etc., provide. Students with poor vision will respond best to bold, bright colors; large shapes; and heavy lines. Care should be taken that they work in well-lighted areas.

# The Studio Curriculum

The studio curriculum consists of forty lessons, and these vary from those that can be completed within a single class period to those that require several class periods. Clearly, there are more lessons provided than are needed for an entire year's program. This was done so that teachers could select from a pool of lessons those that seem most likely to meet the needs, interests, and abilities of their particular students. Also, it was felt that some teachers, on occasion, might wish to have a portion of their classes working on one lesson while the remainder worked on another. For this reason, it was felt that additional lessons were warranted. In any event, providing more lessons than necessary was viewed as one way of adding flexibility to the studio curriculum.

The art lessons which constitute this curriculum are designed to provide students with ample opportunity to develop their creative potential in several important studio areas. These studio areas consist of the following:
- Ceramics.
- Crafts.
- Design.
- Drawing.
- Painting.
- Printmaking.
- Sculpture.

An introductory experience in photography has also been included in this resource book as an expansion of the painting lesson dealing with Impressionism (Lesson 16–2).

The following outline indicates the lessons pertaining to each of these studio areas. These lessons involve students in a variety of experiences which emphasize different subject matter, art elements and principles, media, and techniques.

## Ceramics Experiences:
| | | |
|---|---|---|
| Lesson 6–2 | Functional Coil Vases |
| Lesson 6–3 | Clay Slab Pitcher with Sgraffito Design |
| Lesson 8–1 | Making Ceramic Tesserae |

## Craft Experiences:
| | | |
|---|---|---|
| Lesson 3–3 | A Nonobjective Composition with an Emphasis on Expressive Qualities (Papier Collé) |
| Lesson 8–2 | Using Ceramic Tesserae to Make Mosaic Wall Plaques |
| Lesson 17–2 | Tempera Batik in the Style of Gauguin |

## Design Experiences:
| | | |
|---|---|---|
| Lesson 9–1 | Crayon Etching in the Style of Romanesque Manuscript Illustrations |
| Lesson 12–2 | Designing a Visual Symbol |
| Lesson 13–1 | Bizarre Creatures from Expanded Paper Shapes |

## Drawing Experiences:
| | | |
|---|---|---|
| Lesson 5–2 | Designing a Sarcophagus Cover in the Egyptian Style |
| Lesson 6–1 | Drawings of Buildings with Greek Features |
| Lesson 7–1 | Drawing Exterior Views of Buildings—As They Are |
| Lesson 7–2 | Drawing Exterior Views of Buildings—As They Could Be |
| Lesson 10–2 | Drawing Personal Tympana |
| Lesson 12–1 | Expanding Detail Drawing |
| Lesson 14–1 | Drawing a Shape Moving in Space |
| Lesson 14–2 | Ink Drawings Emphasizing Value Contrasts for Dramatic Effect |
| Lesson 15–1 | Still-Life Drawing in Pastels |
| Lesson 15–2 | Expressing an Emotion or Mood in an Ink Drawing |
| Lesson 18–1 | Drawing in the Cubist Style |
| Lesson 19–1 | Drawing Expressive Portraits |
| Lesson 19–2 | Coloring Expressive Portraits with Oil Pastels |

## Painting Experiences:
| | | |
|---|---|---|
| Lesson 3–1 | A Still Life with an Emphasis on Literal Qualities |
| Lesson 3–2 | A Still Life with an Emphasis on Visual Qualities |
| Lesson 4–1 | Creating the Appearance of Three Dimensions |
| Lesson 5–1 | Painting with Flat Shapes and Monochromatic Color |
| Lesson 5–3 | Painting a Sarcophagus Cover in the Egyptian Style |
| Lesson 11–1 | Painting a Landscape with Gradations of Value to Emphasize Space |
| Lesson 11–2 | Painting a Landscape with Gradations of Intensity to Emphasize Space |
| Lesson 16–1 | Watercolor Still Life in the Style of Delacroix |

Lesson plans for these Studio Experiences, expanding on the lessons presented in the text, follow on pages 28-109.

---

**A Note on Vocabulary Terms:**
A further note on vocabulary is in order here. Expansion of the student's visual vocabulary is an important part of *Art in Focus*, and of the studio curriculum. All important vocabulary terms included on the lesson-plan "RESPONSE/PRODUCTION" charts are defined in the Glossary of *Art in Focus*. Other important vocabulary words in the lesson plans have also been included in the Glossary, and when this has been done it will be called to the teacher's attention with a note to that effect.

I. TITLE OF THE LESSON: A Still Life with an Emphasis on Literal Qualities

II. DURING THIS LESSON STUDENTS ARE TO ACQUIRE INFORMATION ABOUT THE FOLLOWING:

# LESSON 3–1

| RESPONSE | | | | PRODUCTION | | | | |
|---|---|---|---|---|---|---|---|---|
| Artists or Art Objects | Period or Style | Theories of Art | Aesthetic Qualities | Subject Matter | Elements of Art | Principles of Art | Media | Techniques |
| Vigée-Lebrun  Chardin | | Imita-tionalism | Literal Qualities | Still Life | | | Tempera Paint | Painting |

III. OBJECTIVES:

A. RESPONSE:
Students learn that *imitationalism* is defined as the faithful duplication of objects and events drawn from the real world. They can identify and discuss the *literal qualities* found in works of art by *Vigée-Lebrun* and *Chardin*.

B. PRODUCTION:
Using *tempera paints*, students reproduce on white drawing paper a *still life* consisting of no less than three familiar items. These items will first be drawn and then *painted* as accurately as possible as students concentrate attention on the literal qualities.

IV. VISUALS:

Marie Louise Elisabeth Vigée-Lebrun, *The Marquise de Peze and the Marquise de Rouget with Her Two Children* (Figure 3.11)

Jean-Baptiste Siméon Chardin, *Still Life with Rib of Beef* (Figure 15.4)

V. MATERIALS AND TOOLS NEEDED FOR THIS LESSON:

Pencils
White drawing paper (23 × 30.5 cm [9 × 12″])
Tempera paint (see Safety Note in text, page 62)
Brushes
Mixing trays
Paint cloths
Water containers

VI. PRESENTATION OF THE LESSON:

A. Using imitationalist theory as a guide, students discuss the literal qualities noted in a portrait of Vigée-Lebrun and a still life by Chardin. Students are reminded that, according to imitationalism, fine art is defined as the faithful duplication of objects or events drawn from the real world.

B. A still life composed of at least three familiar items is arranged and drawn as accurately as possible on white drawing paper by each student.

C. Using tempera paint, students next paint their still lifes. Concern is again directed towards making their pictures as realistic as possible.

D. When all the paintings are completed, they are placed on display and compared with the still-life arrangements. Initial discussion is limited to the literal qualities. Eventually, however, the teacher asks students if they think the discussion is too limiting—what other aesthetic qualities can be found in the paintings that could also be discussed? In response, students might begin commenting about the colors, lines, shapes, and textures employed in the paintings. They might also note how these elements of art are organized in the various works. Such a discussion would lead into an introduction of the next studio problem, which would deal with the visual qualities stressed by formalism.

VII. EVALUATION OF THE LESSON:
   A. RESPONSE:
      Did students recognize that *imitationalism* stresses the importance of the literal qualities when determining a work's effectiveness? Could they identify and discuss the *literal qualities* found in works of art by *Vigée-Lebrun* and *Chardin*?

   B. PRODUCTION:
      Were the finished *still lifes* drawn and *painted* realistically in *tempera paint* indicating that students had concentrated on the literal qualities?

I. TITLE OF THE LESSON: A Still Life with an Emphasis on Visual Qualities

II. DURING THIS LESSON STUDENTS ARE TO ACQUIRE INFORMATION ABOUT THE FOLLOWING:

# LESSON 3–2

| RESPONSE | | | | PRODUCTION | | | | |
|---|---|---|---|---|---|---|---|---|
| Artists or Art Objects | Period or Style | Theories of Art | Aesthetic Qualities | Subject Matter | Elements of Art | Principles of Art | Media | Techniques |
| Matisse<br><br>Braque | | Formalism | Visual Qualities | Still Life | Elements and Principles Used Are Determined by Individual Students | | Tempera (or Acrylic) Paint | Painting |

III. OBJECTIVES:

A. RESPONSE:

Students learn that *formalism* is defined as the effective organization of the elements and principles of art. Using a Design Chart (page 37 of the text and reproduced on page 119 of this resource book) as a guide, students can identify and discuss the *visual qualities* found in works of art by *Matisse* and *Braque.*

B. PRODUCTION:

Using *tempera paint,** students will *paint* a *still life* consisting of no less than three familiar items. Rather than seek literal accuracy in these paintings, they will be guided by decisions made regarding the selection and use of the *elements* and *principles of art.* Referring to a Design Chart, they identify at least five design relationships which will be employed in their paintings.

IV. VISUALS:

Henri Matisse, *Young Girl Seated* (Figure 3.12)
Georges Braque, *Blue Guitar* (Figure 18.13)

V. MATERIALS AND TOOLS NEEDED FOR THIS LESSON:

Pencils
White drawing paper or canvas board (no less than 23 × 30.5 cm [9 × 12″])
Tempera (or acrylic) paint
Brushes
Paint cloths
Water containers
Mixing trays

VI. PRESENTATION OF THE LESSON:

A. Using formalist theory as a guide, students discuss the visual qualities noted in the paintings by Matisse and Braque. This discussion might focus upon the various design relationships suggested by the Design Chart illustrated on page 37 of the text. Students are reminded that, according to formalism, the most important thing about a work of art is the effective organization of the elements of art through the use of the principles. A striking feature of formalist theory is its disregard for the literal qualities.

B. Referring again to the Design Chart, students are asked to identify no less than five design relationships they wish to concentrate on while completing a painting. Each student is asked to make his or her own decisions with regard to these five design relationships.

C. Students redraw and paint the same still-life arrangement used in the preceding lesson. However, attention is now directed to the visual qualities as students adhere to the decisions made on their Design Charts. For example, a student might opt to use contrasting thick and thin lines, repeat certain curvilinear shapes, and select a color scheme

---

*Acrylic paints may be used in this painting lesson.

made up of a complex assortment of hues, intensities, and values. (These terms have been included in the text glossary.)

D. When completed, the paintings are placed on display and compared to the actual still-life arrangement and to each other. Even though all students paint the same subject, their paintings will be found to differ, sometimes quite dramatically. Differences will be traced back to individual decisions made on the Design Chart, decisions which determined how the elements and principles of art would be used.

VII. EVALUATION OF THE LESSON:

A. RESPONSE:

Did students recognize that *formalism* stresses the importance of the visual qualities when determining a work's effectiveness? Using a Design Chart as a guide, could they identify and discuss the *visual qualities* found in works of art by *Matisse* and *Braque?*

B. PRODUCTION:

Did students *paint* a *still life* with *tempera* that consisted of no less than three items? Did the completed paintings demonstrate that students adhered to the five decisions made on the Design Chart concerning the use of the *elements* and *principles of art?*

I. TITLE OF THE LESSON: A Nonobjective Composition with an Emphasis on Expressive Qualities

II. DURING THIS LESSON STUDENTS ARE TO ACQUIRE INFORMATION ABOUT THE FOLLOWING:

# LESSON 3–3

| RESPONSE | | | | PRODUCTION | | | | |
|---|---|---|---|---|---|---|---|---|
| Artists or Art Objects | Period or Style | Theories of Art | Aesthetic Qualities | Subject Matter | Elements of Art | Principles of Art | Media | Techniques |
| Guglielmi Kandinsky | | Emotional-ism | Expressive Qualities | | Shape | Emphasis (Center of Interest) | Mixed Media | Papier Collé (Collage) |

III. OBJECTIVES:

A. RESPONSE:

Students learn that *emotionalism* is defined as the vivid communication of ideas, moods, and feelings. They can identify and discuss the *expressive qualities* found in works of art by *Guglielmi* and *Kandinsky*.

B. PRODUCTION:

Using *mixed media* (watercolor, torn magazine illustrations, and glue), students complete a nonobjective *papier collé*, or "collage," that communicates a one-word idea, such as lost, lonely, happy, hate, love, pain. Torn magazine *shapes* are to be arranged to *emphasize* a center of interest in the composition. (Both "nonobjective" and "collage" are defined in the *Art in Focus* Glossary.)

IV. VISUALS:

Louis Guglielmi, *Terror in Brooklyn* (Figure 3.13)

Vasily Kandinsky, *Improvisation 28* (Figure 18.8)

V. MATERIALS AND TOOLS NEEDED FOR THIS LESSON:

Poster board (30.5 × 46 cm [12 × 18″])
Glue (see Safety Note in text, page 242)
Watercolors
Watercolor brushes
Pages torn from magazines, newspapers, etc.
Water containers
Paint cloths

VI. PRESENTATION OF THE LESSON:

A. Using emotionalist theory as a guide, students discuss the expressive qualities noted in the paintings by Guglielmi and Kandinsky.

B. Students select a one-word idea as the theme for a papier collé.* They then tear pages from magazines and newspapers which contain images, words, or colors associated with this idea.

C. A variety of large and small irregular shapes torn from the magazine and newspaper pages are carefully arranged on a sheet of poster board. This arrangement should aim at achieving a focal point or center of interest for the composition. When this is accomplished, the shapes are glued in place.

D. Opaque and transparent applications of watercolor paint are used to dull or tone down some areas and highlight other areas in these compositions. In this manner, students can further accent their centers of interest while completing nonobjective works which subtly communicate a one-word message to viewers.

E. Several layers of paper and watercolor paint are often required before an acceptable finished surface is realized.

F. When the works are completed, each is displayed by the student-artist, and other members of the class attempt to identify the one-word message.

---

*The teacher may choose to complete a number of small cards on which different ideas are written. These could be placed in a bag or box and passed around the room so that each student may reach in and blindly select one.

## VII. EVALUATION OF THE LESSON:

### A. RESPONSE:

Did students recognize that *emotionalism* stresses the importance of the expressive qualities when determining a work's effectiveness? Could they identify and discuss the *expressive qualities* found in works of art by *Guglielmi* and *Kandinsky*?

### B. PRODUCTION:

Did the *papier collé* compositions succeed in communicating a one-word idea to others, demonstrating that students had effectively directed their attention to the expressive qualities? Were the shapes arranged to emphasize a center of interest in the composition? Were the nonobjective works completed using the *mixed media* specified?

# LESSON 3–3 (Continued)

**Nonobjective papier collé (secondary-level student work)**

I. TITLE OF THE LESSON: Creating the Appearance of Three Dimensions

II. DURING THIS LESSON STUDENTS ARE TO ACQUIRE INFORMATION ABOUT THE FOLLOWING:

# LESSON 4–1

| RESPONSE | | | | PRODUCTION | | | | |
|---|---|---|---|---|---|---|---|---|
| Artists or Art Objects | Period or Style | Theories of Art | Aesthetic Qualities | Subject Matter | Elements of Art | Principles of Art | Media | Techniques |
| Bison, Altamira  Deer, Altamira | Prehistoric Art | | | Animals | Value (Color) | Gradation | Tempera Paint | Painting |

III. OBJECTIVES:

A. RESPONSE:

Students learn that *prehistoric* artists tried to make their painted animals look as lifelike as possible. They can point out the gradual changes of value in paintings of a *bison* and a *deer from Altamira* and explain that this was done to create the impression of a three-dimensional form projecting outward from a wall or ceiling.

B. PRODUCTION:

Each student will complete a large, simple contour drawing of an *animal* of his or her own choosing. This drawing will fill completely a 30.5 × 46-cm [12 × 18-inch] sheet of white drawing paper. Students will then select a single *tempera* color and *paint* their animal using *gradation* of *value* in such a manner that the animal will appear three-dimensional. Gradations of value will be secured by adding white or black tempera to the single color selected.

IV. VISUALS:

*Bison,* Altamira (Figure 4.1)
*Deer,* Altamira (Figure 4.5)

V. MATERIALS AND TOOLS NEEDED FOR THIS LESSON:

Pencils
White drawing paper (30.5 × 46 cm [12 × 18″])
Tempera paint
Brushes
Mixing trays
Paint cloths
Water containers

VI. PRESENTATION OF THE LESSON:

A. Students examine and discuss the paintings of a bison and a deer from Altamira, noting how gradation of value was used to make these animals look more three-dimensional and lifelike.

B. Following the discussion, students complete a large contour drawing of an animal in pencil which fills completely a sheet of white drawing paper. This drawing should be relatively simple, without unnecessary details.

C. Selecting a single hue and adding white or black to alter its value, students then paint their animals with tempera.* A gradual change from dark to light and light to dark values will be employed as students attempt to create the impression of a solid, three-dimensional animal form.

D. Details and accents may be added with black paint.

E. Finished paintings are displayed and discussed in terms of their effectiveness in creating the illusion of three-dimensional forms.

---

*This same Studio Experience can be presented by substituting pastels or charcoal. (If this is done, see Safety Note in text, page 281.)

VII. EVALUATION OF THE LESSON:
  A. RESPONSE:
     Were students able to recognize that *prehistoric* paintings, such as the *Bison* and *Deer from Altamira*, were painted with gradual changes of value to make them look as lifelike as possible?
  B. PRODUCTION:
     Did each student complete a large *tempera* painting of an *animal* and *paint* it with *gradations* of *value* to give it a three-dimensional appearance? Was only one color used, and were gradations of value secured by adding black or white tempera?

# LESSON 4–1 (Continued)

I. TITLE OF THE LESSON: Modeling a Three-Dimensional Animal in Clay

II. DURING THIS LESSON STUDENTS ARE TO ACQUIRE INFORMATION ABOUT THE FOLLOWING:

# LESSON 4–2

| RESPONSE | | | | PRODUCTION | | | | |
|---|---|---|---|---|---|---|---|---|
| Artists or Art Objects | Period or Style | Theories of Art | Aesthetic Qualities | Subject Matter | Elements of Art | Principles of Art | Media | Techniques |
| Bison, Altamira<br><br>Deer, Altamira | Prehistoric Art | | | Animals | Form (Geometric)<br><br>Texture (Actual) | | Clay | Modeling |

III. OBJECTIVES:
A. RESPONSE:
Students recognize that *prehistoric* artists attempted to reproduce the traits or characteristics associated with the animals they painted. They are able to identify these traits as evidenced in paintings of a *bison* and a *deer from Altamira*.

B. PRODUCTION:
Each student will *model** in *clay* a compact *animal* sculpture based on one of the basic *geometric forms* (sphere, cylinder, cone). This animal sculpture will be enhanced with *actual textures* scratched or stamped into the clay surface. It will also depict a particular trait (powerful, graceful, gentle) associated with that animal.

IV. VISUALS:
*Bison,* Altamira (Figure 4.1)
*Deer,* Altamira (Figure 4.5)

*Students should be made aware that sculptures can be created by employing one or more forming processes. These forming processes are as follows:
1. Modeling—a manipulative/additive process
2. Carving—a subtractive process (see Lesson 10–3)
3. Construction—an additive process (see Lessons 18–3 and 19–3)

V. MATERIALS AND TOOLS NEEDED FOR THIS LESSON:

Pencils
Newsprint (for sketching)
Clay (a ball about the size of a grapefruit) (see Safety Note in text, page 71)
Clay-modeling tools ("Modeling tools" defined in text Glossary)
Slip (defined in text Glossary)
Sections of burlap (about 36 × 36 cm [14 × 14"]) for each student to use in covering table tops
Various instruments used to scratch or stamp a texture into soft clay

VI. PRESENTATION OF THE LESSON:
A. Students examine the paintings of a bison and a deer from Altamira and discuss the ways the artists succeeded in showing the animals' power, grace, and gentleness. The students are then asked to compile a list of different animals that have these same traits. At the chalkboard, the teacher lists each animal named under the appropriate trait. For example, under "gentleness" might be listed "deer," "kitten," "lamb."

B. Each student selects one of the animals listed on the board and prepares a pencil sketch of it in a compact reclining or sitting position. These sketches should attempt to reveal the trait associated with each animal.

C. Using the sketches as guides, students model the animal in clay, adhering to the following procedure:
1. They first identify and fashion in clay a geometric form that most closely resembles the body of the animal in their sketches. Typical forms include the sphere, cylinder, and cone.

2. The head, legs, tail, and other large features are added to the basic geometric form to construct the animal. Compactness is sought to maintain the integrity of the simple geometric form. (The teacher should demonstrate how students are to join pieces of clay together by roughing up or "scoring" the surfaces, adding slip, and pressing the pieces firmly together.)

3. Students are reminded to keep turning the sculpture rather than working on it from one side. Once the larger features have been joined to the basic form, details can be added and actual textures applied. Various instruments can be used to scratch or stamp a texture into the clay that will resemble hair or fur.

4. Students should be instructed to gather all parts of the animal into a unifying whole, a compact mass.

5. When the clay pieces are firm enough to allow it, they are hollowed out from the bottom, allowed to dry thoroughly, and kiln fired.

   (Safety Note: Kiln firing will create a safety hazard unless proper measures are taken for adequate ventilation of the room in which the kiln is being used. Toxic fumes result from firing and are best eliminated through a special ventilation device, such as a canopy hood. Also see "Safety in the Art Studio," page 110 of this *Teacher's Resource Book,* for more safety information regarding use of a kiln.

## VII. EVALUATION OF THE LESSON:

### A. RESPONSE:

Did students recognize that *prehistoric* animal paintings revealed the traits or characteristics associated with those animals? Were students able to identify those traits in paintings of a *bison* and a *deer from Altamira?*

### B. PRODUCTION:

Were the *animal* sculptures students *modeled* in *clay* based on one of the basic *geometric forms?* Did they apply *actual textures* to the clay surfaces? Did the finished clay animals reveal a trait commonly associated with those animals?

**Animal sculpture (secondary-level student work)**

I. TITLE OF THE LESSON: Painting with Flat Shapes and Monochromatic Color

II. DURING THIS LESSON STUDENTS ARE TO ACQUIRE INFORMATION ABOUT THE FOLLOWING:

# LESSON 5–1

| RESPONSE | | | | PRODUCTION | | | | |
|---|---|---|---|---|---|---|---|---|
| Artists or Art Objects | Period or Style | Theories of Art | Aesthetic Qualities | Subject Matter | Elements of Art | Principles of Art | Media | Techniques |
| Egyptian Wall Paintings, Tomb of Nakht | Style of Ancient Egypt | | | Houses | Shape Color (Hue) Space (to be avoided) | Harmony | Tempera Paint | Painting |

III. OBJECTIVES:

A. RESPONSE:
When viewing several works of art representing various periods and places, students are able to identify correctly those done by ancient Egyptian artists. Further, students are able to explain that the *Egyptian painting style,* as exemplified by the *wall paintings from the Tomb of Nakht,* is recognizable because it ignores space and stresses the two-dimensional arrangement of flat shapes.

B. PRODUCTION:
Emulating the Egyptian painting style, students use *tempera* to *paint* pictures of *houses* in which flat *shapes* are organized in a two-dimensional design. No attempt is made to indicate distance or *space* in these paintings. A simple, *monochromatic color* scheme is employed to increase overall *harmony.* ("Monochromatic" is defined in text Glossary.)

IV. VISUALS:

Wall painting from the Tomb of Nakht: *Ceremonial Door* (Figure 5.11)

Wall painting from the Tomb of Nakht: *Nakht and His Wife* (Figure 5.12)

Comparisons can be made to the following works:

*Annunciation,* Illustration from a Swabian Gospel Manuscript (Figure 9.24)

The Limbourg Brothers, *May,* a page from a book of hours painted for the Duke of Berry (Figure 10.17)

Duccio, *The Calling of the Apostles Peter and Andrew* (Figure 10.19)

Giotto, *Lamentation* (Figure 10.20)

Masaccio, *The Tribute Money* (Figure 11.3)

V. MATERIALS AND TOOLS NEEDED FOR THIS LESSON:

Pencils
Newsprint
White drawing paper (23 × 30.5 cm [9 × 12″])
Tempera paint
Brushes
Mixing trays
Paint cloths
Water containers

VI. PRESENTATION OF THE LESSON:

A. Several paintings, including two from the tomb of Nakht in Egypt, are viewed and discussed in class.* Students are asked to point to the features noted in the ancient Egyptian paintings that distinguish them from works created at other times and in other places. As a consequence, they observe that the Egyptian paintings are characterized by a lack of space. Space is eliminated in favor of a two-dimensional arrangement of flat shapes. Figures and objects are placed side by side or vertically above one another to create a flat, decorative design.

---

*It is suggested that, in addition to the Egyptian wall paintings, students view artworks in which deep space is emphasized. Paintings by Renaissance artists would be well suited for this purpose, for example, Masaccio's *The Tribute Money* (Figure 11.3), Uccello's *The Battle of San Romano,* (Figure 11.8), Botticelli's *The Adoration of the Magi* (Figure 11.4), and Raphael's *The Alba Madonna* (Figure 11.21).

B. Students are asked to complete several pencil sketches of houses. Each of these sketches will include no less than six houses.

C. On a piece of white paper, students redraw the best of their sketches but eliminate any indication of three-dimensional space. Finished line drawings will exhibit no perspective (defined in text Glossary), overlapping, or size differences. Houses and other objects (trees, telephone poles, sidewalks, signs) are shown as though they are all on the same plane. Some students may choose to arrange their houses vertically above one another to fill the entire piece of paper.

D. The drawings are then painted in a monochromatic color scheme to achieve a harmonious composition.

   1. Each student selects a color and mixes it with white, black, and its complement to create a variety of tints and shades.

   2. The paint is applied evenly to further emphasize the flat quality of the shapes.

   3. Textural effects and details may be added by using a fine brush and black or white paint.

   4. Throughout the painting process, students are reminded that their compositions are to emphasize the two-dimensional placement of flat shapes. All efforts to create the illusion of space should be avoided.

# LESSON 5–1 (Continued)

VII. EVALUATION OF THE LESSON:

   A. RESPONSE:
   Were students able to explain that the *Egyptian painting style* is distinguished from other painting styles viewed in class because it ignores space and stresses the two-dimensional arrangement of flat shapes? Were they able to identify these features of Egyptian art in the *wall paintings from the Tomb of Nakht?*

   B. PRODUCTION:
   Did the *houses* students *paint*ed with *tempera* incorporate flat *shapes* organized in a two-dimensional design? Were the students successful in eliminating all suggestions of distance or *space?* Did they employ a simple, *monochromatic color* scheme to increase overall *harmony* in the work?

I. TITLE OF THE LESSON: Designing a Sarcophagus Cover in the Egyptian Style

II. DURING THIS LESSON STUDENTS ARE TO ACQUIRE INFORMATION ABOUT THE FOLLOWING:

# LESSON 5-2

| RESPONSE | | | | PRODUCTION | | | | |
|---|---|---|---|---|---|---|---|---|
| Artists or Art Objects | Period or Style | Theories of Art | Aesthetic Qualities | Subject Matter | Elements of Art | Principles of Art | Media | Techniques |
| Portrait of Hesire | Style of Ancient Egypt | | | Portrait | | | Pencil | Drawing |

III. OBJECTIVES:

A. RESPONSE:

Students learn that ancient *Egyptian* artists were required to adhere to rigid rules when carving and painting *portraits*. Referring to a relief *Portrait of Hesire* (Figure 5.10), they are able to explain how those rules affected the way this figure was carved, that is, its *style*.

B. PRODUCTION:

Each student will complete no less than two *drawings* in *pencil* which represent designs for coffin lids for a fictional deceased Pharaoh. These designs must do the following:

1. Show how the Pharaoh looked, suggest his personality, and indicate his major accomplishments.
2. Present the head, arms, legs, and feet of the Pharaoh in profile and the eyes and shoulders as viewed from the front.

IV. VISUALS:

*Portrait of Hesire* (Figure 5.10)

V. MATERIALS AND TOOLS NEEDED FOR THIS LESSON:

Pencils
White drawing paper (23 × 30.5 cm [9 × 12″])

VI. PRESENTATION OF THE LESSON:

A. Students reread Chapter 5 of the text and discuss the effect that the religious beliefs had upon ancient Egyptian burial customs. Of major concern is the fact that the mummified remains of Egyptian Pharaohs were sealed in stone coffins called "sarcophagi."

These sarcophagi were then hidden within huge pyramids. In this way it was thought that the Pharaoh's body would be preserved and protected until the eventual return of his ka, or spirit. United with the ka, the Pharaoh's body would then embark on a final journey to the next world.

B. Examining the relief sculpture of Hesire, students observe that the strict rules imposed upon sculptors at that time demanded that all parts of the body be shown from the most familiar points of view. The head, arms, legs, and feet were shown in profile, while the eyes and shoulders were presented as if seen from the front. These rules resulted in the development of a unique Egyptian style of art.

C. The teacher asks the class to imagine that they are living in a culture similar to that of the ancient Egyptians. This culture requires that its Pharaohs be buried in sarcophagi with highly decorated lids. These lids not only provide a picture of the Pharaoh within the sarcophagus, but also tell a great deal about his personality and accomplishments. Moreover, like Egyptian relief sculptures and paintings, these representations of the Pharaoh were always designed so that the head, arms, legs, and feet are in profile and the eyes and shoulders shown as if viewed from the front.

D. The class is divided into three groups. Each group receives a card on which is written the outstanding characteristic of a recently deceased Pharaoh. One group's Pharaoh is characterized as "scholarly," another's as a "tyrant," and the third's as a great "spiritual leader." Each group is told not to share the information on their card with the other groups.

|  | I. SCHOLAR | II. TYRANT | III. SPIRITUAL LEADER |
|---|---|---|---|
| Appearance | 1.<br>2.<br>3.<br>4.<br>5. | 1.<br>2.<br>3.<br>4.<br>5. | 1.<br>2.<br>3.<br>4.<br>5. |
| Personality | 1.<br>2.<br>3.<br>4.<br>5. | 1.<br>2.<br>3.<br>4.<br>5. | 1.<br>2.<br>3.<br>4.<br>5. |
| Accomplishments | 1.<br>2.<br>3.<br>4.<br>5. | 1.<br>2.<br>3.<br>4.<br>5. | 1.<br>2.<br>3.<br>4.<br>5. |

E. Each group of students is given an opportunity to discuss and determine the appearance, personality, and accomplishments of their Pharaoh. The teacher provides a matrix (on the chalkboard or on an overhead transparency) to aid students in making decisions concerning these traits. This matrix might look like the example above. Students in each of the three groups arrive at a mental image of their Pharaoh based upon the decisions made on this matrix.

F. On a sheet of white drawing paper (23 × 30.5 cm [9 × 12″]), each student completes two identical outlines of sarcophagi lids conforming to the measurements shown in Figure 7.

G. Each student then draws a design for both sarcophagi lids. Each of these designs must reflect the following concerns:
1. Present versions of the fictional Pharaoh which will provide viewers with a clear picture of how he looked and what kind of personality he had.
2. Provide clues regarding the Pharaoh's major accomplishments.
3. Adhere to a style in which the head, arms, legs, and feet are always shown in profile, while the eyes and shoulders are shown from the front.

VII. EVALUATION OF THE LESSON:
A. RESPONSE:
Did students understand that ancient *Egyptian* artists were required to adhere to rigid rules when carving and painting *portraits*? Were they able to explain how those rules contributed to the development of a unique *Egyptian style of art?* Could they point out the main characteristics of that style in a relief *Portrait of Hesire?*

B. PRODUCTION:
Did each student complete two or more *drawings* in *pencil* which represent designs for sarcophagi lids for a fictional deceased Pharaoh? Did these designs . . .
1. Show how the king looked, suggest his personality, and indicate his major accomplishments?
2. Present the head, arms, legs, and feet in profile and the eyes and shoulders as viewed from the front?

**Figure 7.**

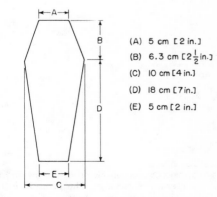

(A) 5 cm [2 in.]
(B) 6.3 cm [2½ in.]
(C) 10 cm [4 in.]
(D) 18 cm [7 in.]
(E) 5 cm [2 in.]

I. TITLE OF THE LESSON: Painting a Sarcophagus Cover in the Egyptian Style*

II. DURING THIS LESSON STUDENTS ARE TO ACQUIRE INFORMATION ABOUT THE FOLLOWING:

# LESSON 5–3

| RESPONSE | | | | PRODUCTION | | | | |
|---|---|---|---|---|---|---|---|---|
| Artists or Art Objects | Period or Style | Theories of Art | Aesthetic Qualities | Subject Matter | Elements of Art | Principles of Art | Media | Techniques |
| | Style of Ancient Egypt | | | Portraits | Hue Intensity Value (Color) Shape | Emphasis Gradation (to be avoided) | Tempera Paint | Painting |

III. OBJECTIVES:

A. RESPONSE:

Students learn that the ancient *Egyptian painting style* was characterized by the use of bright red and yellow hues, with black and blue-green added for contrast. They also observe that little gradation in value was employed in Egyptian paintings. Consequently, the shapes appear flat, as if cut from paper and pasted to the walls of ancient tombs.

B. PRODUCTION:

Each student will select one of the sarcophagi-lid designs completed in the previous lesson and reproduce it on a larger format. These will then be *painted* in *tempera* using contrasting *hues* such as red, yellow, and orange. *Emphasis* will be achieved by using blue-green and black hues. *No gradation* of *value* will be employed as students seek to emphasize the flat quality of the *shapes* used in their *portraits* of a deceased Pharaoh.

IV. VISUALS:

Examine books on Egyptian art to find examples of Egyptian sarcophagi covers. These books should be passed around the room during the discussion portion of the lesson.

V. MATERIALS AND TOOLS NEEDED FOR THIS LESSON:

Sketches completed in the previous lesson
Pencils
Poster board (one 46 × 61-cm [18 × 24-inch] sheet for two students)
Tempera paint
Brushes
Mixing trays
Paint cloths
Water containers

VI. PRESENTATION OF THE LESSON:

A. Students examine several examples of Egyptian painting presented by the teacher. In answer to the teacher's questions, they observe that these paintings are often characterized by intense red and yellow hues with blue-green and black added for contrast. They also note that the shapes in these paintings appear to be flat because no gradation in value was used.

B. Students are asked to select the best of the two sarcophagi lids completed in the previous lesson. Larger versions of these sarcophagi-lid designs are reproduced on 23 × 61-cm [9 × 24-inch] sections of poster board.* Measurements for the larger sarcophagi lids are provided in Figure 8.

---

*The sarcophagi covers completed in this lesson may also serve as designs for clay relief carvings. The procedure for completing a clay relief carving is outlined in Lesson 10–3.

*By cutting a sheet of 46 × 61-cm [18 × 24-inch] poster board in half, lengthwise sections for two students are obtained.

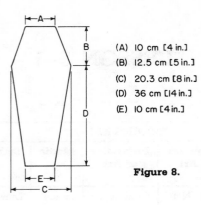

(A) 10 cm [4 in.]
(B) 12.5 cm [5 in.]
(C) 20.3 cm [8 in.]
(D) 36 cm [14 in.]
(E) 10 cm [4 in.]

**Figure 8.**

C. Using tempera, students paint their designs, making certain to use intense reds, yellows, and oranges. Blue-green and black are added for contrast. Shapes are painted without gradation of value in order to replicate the flat quality noted in Egyptian paintings.

D. When completed, students exhibit their paintings in groups. Each group in turn then tries to determine as much as possible about the Pharaohs represented on the other groups' sarcophagi lids. The matrix used in the preceding lesson might be used as a guide here as each group seeks to learn as much as they can about the appearance, personality, and accomplishments of the other groups' Pharaohs.

VII. EVALUATION OF THE LESSON:

A. RESPONSE:

Were students able to point to the use of intense hues and the lack of value gradation as characteristics of the *Egyptian painting style*? Did they also reveal that the lack of value gradation contributed to the overall flat appearance of these paintings?

B. PRODUCTION:

Did each student complete a *painting* in *tempera* which made use of *intense* red, yellow, and orange *hues*? Was *emphasis* obtained by adding contrasting blue-green and black hues? Did students avoid *gradation* in *value* to achieve a flat quality in their *shapes*? Were the finished paintings *portraits* of a deceased Pharaoh?

**Egyptian-style sarcophagus cover (secondary-level student work)**

I. TITLE OF THE LESSON: Drawings of Buildings wih Greek Features

II. DURING THIS LESSON STUDENTS ARE TO ACQUIRE INFORMATION ABOUT THE FOLLOWING:

# LESSON 6–1

| RESPONSE | | | | PRODUCTION | | | | |
|---|---|---|---|---|---|---|---|---|
| Artists or Art Objects | Period or Style | Theories of Art | Aesthetic Qualities | Subject Matter | Elements of Art | Principles of Art | Media | Techniques |
| Examples of Greek Architecture | Greek Style of Architecture | | | Buildings or Parts of Buildings | Value (Non-Color) | Gradation Emphasis | Pencil | Drawing |

III. OBJECTIVES:

A. RESPONSE:

Students learn to identify the features of *Greek* architecture, including posts and lintels, sloping or gabled roofs, colonnades, capitals, and stylobates. They are also able to name the decorative orders,* can point to the differences between them, and can identify them when found on various *examples of Greek architecture.*

B. PRODUCTION:

Students complete detailed, accurate *pencil drawings* of *buildings or parts of buildings* in their community that incorporate features of Greek architecture. *Value gradation* will be used to add to the three-dimensional quality of these drawings. Contrasts of value will be used to add *emphasis* to the most important parts of each drawing.

IV. VISUALS:

Parthenon (Figure 6.1)
Greek Orders (Figure 6.5)
Temple of Athena Nike (Figure 6.6)
Erechtheum (Figure 6.7)
Monument to Lysicrates (Figure 6.8)

V. MATERIALS AND TOOLS NEEDED FOR THIS LESSON:

Pencils
Newsprint
White drawing paper (23 × 30 cm [9 × 12″] or larger)

VI. PRESENTATION OF THE LESSON:

A. Students examine examples of Greek architecture and, on the chalkboard, compile a list of their features. The discussion of Greek architecture also includes a consideration of the decorative orders, and students identify each as they appear on the buildings studied.

B. An out-of-class assignment requires that students search their community for examples of buildings or parts of buildings that exhibit an obvious Greek influence.

C. Preliminary sketches of the buildings or parts of buildings are made on the spot. These preliminary sketches are referred to in class when final detailed pencil drawings are done. When working on these final drawings, students are urged to direct their attention to both accuracy and detail. Value gradation is used to enhance the three-dimensional quality of their drawings.* The most important parts of each drawing will be emphasized by using bold contrasts of value.

---

*The Greek decorative orders, Doric, Ionic, and Corinthian, are discussed in the text, Chapter 6, pages 92-94.

---

*Students can use dots, lines, diagonal shading, crosshatching, or individualized linear patterns to create a range of values (and textures) in these drawings (terms defined in text Glossary).

VIII. EVALUATION OF THE LESSON:
  A. RESPONSE:
     Were students able to identify correctly the features of *Greek* architecture? Could they name the decorative orders, point to the differences between them, and identify them when found on various *examples of Greek architecture?*
  B. PRODUCTION:
     Did students complete detailed, accurate *pencil drawings* of *buildings or parts of buildings* in their community that incorporate features of Greek architecture? Did they use *value gradation* to add to the three-dimensional quality of these drawings? Were contrasts of value used to *emphasize* the most important parts of each drawing?

# LESSON 6–1 (Continued)

I. TITLE OF THE LESSON: Functional Coil Vases

II. DURING THIS LESSON STUDENTS ARE TO ACQUIRE INFORMATION ABOUT THE FOLLOWING:

# LESSON 6–2

| RESPONSE | | | | PRODUCTION | | | | |
|---|---|---|---|---|---|---|---|---|
| Artists or Art Objects | Period or Style | Theories of Art | Aesthetic Qualities | Subject Matter | Elements of Art | Principles of Art | Media | Techniques |
| Greek Vessels | Ancient Greece | | | Vase | Form<br><br>Texture (Actual) | Balance (Symmetrical) | Clay | Coil Construction |

III. OBJECTIVES:

A. RESPONSE:

Students learn that in *ancient Greece a variety of vessel* forms were developed.* These forms were completely functional, since the vessels were designed to serve specific purposes.

B. PRODUCTION:

Students will complete a *clay vase* using the *coil method of construction*. Each vase will be at least 25.4 cm [10″] tall, be *symmetrically balanced*, and exhibit a rich, overall *texture*. The *form* of each vase will take into account the vessel's intended function.

IV. VISUALS:

*Geometric Jug* (Figure 6.20)
*Vase* from the Diplyon cemetery (Figure 6.21)
Exekias, *Vase with Ajax and Achilles Playing Draughts* (Figure 6.22)

---

*Greek vases were designed to serve different functions and their shapes reflected these functions. Vases were intended to serve as drinking vessels, water jars, oil flasks, bowls for mixing beverages, and storage containers for wine, oil, honey, and grain.

V. MATERIALS AND TOOLS NEEDED FOR THIS LESSON:

Pencils
Newsprint
Cardboard (for templates)
Pieces of cloth, burlap, or canvas
Wood slats (1 cm [⅜″] thick)
Water-base clay
Slip
Slip containers
Modeling tools
Rolling pins
Combs

VI. PRESENTATION OF THE LESSON:

A. Several Greek vases are examined with concern directed to the forms of those vases. Students observe that these vases are completely functional; that is, they were designed for specific purposes.

B. Students are asked to make a number of vase outlines on newsprint. These vases must be designed with a specific purpose in mind.

C. Completed outlines are displayed on the bulletin board, and the class discusses the various forms suggested in terms of the art principles observed. Thus a slender, lithe form might be contrasted with the more stable qualities of a broad, heavy-based form, or a simple form might be compared to another which is complex. (It is important here that students realize that the basic silhouette, or outline, will determine to a large extent the function as well as the appearance of the vase.)

D. Each student selects the most appealing of his or her outlines and prepares a cardboard template (defined in text Glossary) of it. When cut out, these templates should measure no less than 25.4 cm [10″] in height.

E. Clay slabs of uniform thickness are prepared using a rolling pin to flatten a ball of clay placed between two 1-cm [⅜-inch] thick wood slats.

F. A circular piece is cut from each clay slab to serve as a base for the vase.

G. Three or four coils of clay are rolled out so that each is about 1 cm [⅜″] in diameter. (Sometimes, when rolling, a coil will become flattened. When this happens, the coil should be patted back into shape before the student continues rolling.)

H. Coils are connected to the circular base and to each other with a coat of slip (liquid clay) after the surfaces have been roughened with a comb. (Roughing the surfaces and coating them with slip helps the coils adhere to the base and to each other.)

I. After each coil is put into place, it is cut to size with an angle cut. The two ends are joined together and the coil is fastened to the one below by using a modeling tool. By using different tools and varying the spacing of the tool marks, different textural effects can be realized.

J. After each coil is locked in place, students should place their cardboard templates along the clay wall. If the fit is not right, the clay wall should be adjusted. At the same time, students should be advised to check the vase for roundness.

K. If the clay wall begins to sag as the building progresses, it is necessary to set the vase aside until the clay has hardened enough to support the weight.

L. The final, top coil should be as round as possible and placed carefully so that it will be circular. Before this is done, students should be reminded that their vases must be no less than 25.4 cm [10″] tall.

# LESSON 6–2 (Continued)

M. When the vase is leather-hard, a sponge may be used to eliminate any hard edges and to shape up the lip of the vase.

N. When completely dry, the vase is bisque fired* and glazed.**

VII. EVALUATION OF THE LESSON:
A. RESPONSE:
Did students acknowledge that a *variety of vessel forms* were developed in *ancient Greece?* Did they understand that these vessels were completely functional and were designed to serve specific purposes?

B. PRODUCTION:
Did students employ the *coil method of construction* to construct a *clay vase?* Were these vases at least 25.4 cm [10″] tall, *symmetrically balanced,* and created with a rich, overall *texture?* Did the form of each vase take into account the vessel's intended function?

---

*Clay pieces should be allowed to dry slowly and thoroughly before being fired in a kiln. Artificial heat applied to speed the drying time is likely to cause the pieces to crack.

---

**Non-lead* glazes should be used. (See Safety Note in text, page 107.)

I. TITLE OF THE LESSON: Clay Slab Pitcher with Sgraffito Design

II. DURING THIS LESSON STUDENTS ARE TO ACQUIRE INFORMATION ABOUT THE FOLLOWING:

# LESSON 6–3

| RESPONSE | | | | PRODUCTION | | | | |
|---|---|---|---|---|---|---|---|---|
| Artists or Art Objects | Period or Style | Theories of Art | Aesthetic Qualities | Subject Matter | Elements of Art | Principles of Art | Media | Techniques |
| Exekias | Ancient Greece | Formalism | Visual Qualities | Pitcher | Line  Form | Variety | Clay | Slab Construction |

III. OBJECTIVES:

A. RESPONSE:

Examining an *ancient Greek* vase by *Exekias,* students use *formalism* as a guide to its *visual qualities.* They are able to explain how the scene on the vase is designed to complement the shape of the vessel. They point to the way the figures lean forward and the manner in which the lines of their backs curve to repeat the curve of the vase. They also note how the lines of the spears continue the lines of the handles and lead the viewer's eye to the center of the composition.

B. PRODUCTION:

Students design and complete a *clay slab pitcher* with a handle and spout. The pitcher is decorated with a sgraffito *line* pattern consisting of a *variety* of thick and thin lines. This sgraffito design complements the *form* of the vessel upon which it is placed.

IV. VISUALS:

Exekias, *Vase with Ajax and Achilles Playing Draughts* (Figure 6.22)

V. MATERIALS AND TOOLS NEEDED FOR THIS LESSON:

Pencils
Newsprint
Water-base clay
Slip or engobe* (of a different color than the water-base clay above)
Wood slats (0.6 cm [¼″] thick)
Rolling pins
Fettling knives (defined in text Glossary)
Brushes (to use in applying engobe)
Incising tools (for scratching designs in the engobe)
Pieces of cloth, burlap, or canvas

VI. PRESENTATION OF THE LESSON:

A. The Greek vase by Exekias is examined and students note the ways in which the decorative design reflects and complements the shape of the vessel.

B. Students are informed that they will complete a clay slab pitcher which will have a sgraffito** design. They are challenged to create a linear design which will, like the design on the Exekias vase, take into account the unique shapes of their pitchers.

C. Full-size paper patterns are prepared which, when formed into a cylinder, approximate the size and shape of the pitchers. Students are encouraged to experiment with various shapes until they arrive at the ones that are most pleasing. Each design, however, must include a pouring spout and a handle.

D. The paper pattern is placed over a slab of clay rolled out to a uniform 1.3-cm [½-inch] thickness. (The slab is prepared by using a rolling pin to flatten a ball of clay placed between two 0.6-cm [¼-inch] thick wood slats.) The shape for the pitcher is cut from the clay slab with a fettling knife.

---

*Slip and engobe are actually the same material—a fluid mixture of water and clay. However, when slip is used for decorative purposes, it is generally called an "engobe." (Both terms are defined in the text Glossary.)

---

**Sgraffito involves an engraving process in which a clay piece is first coated with an engobe and then scratched through, revealing the clay body beneath. The engobe used in this process is always a different color than the clay body on which it is applied. ("Sgraffito" is defined in the text Glossary.)

E. The clay is allowed to stiffen slightly. It is then placed in an upright position and folded carefully to form an oval shape. The two ends of the clay slab are pinched firmly together to close the form and provide the material needed for the handle.

F. The inside seam is sealed securely with a coil of clay which is worked into place with the fingers, a wooden modeling tool, or a pointed pencil.

G. The pitcher is placed upright on another 1.3- cm [½-inch] slab of clay and the bottom shape traced and cut from it. The bottom edge of the pitcher and the top of the slab bottom are scored, slip is applied, and the pieces are joined together. For added strength, a clay coil may be added to the inside seam and blended in place with a modeling tool. The outside of the pitcher is then smoothed off.

H. The handle is outlined on the clay with a pointed pencil. Excess clay is cut off with a fettling knife to form the outer shape of the handle. The handle opening is marked and cut out in the same manner, as shown in Figure 9. It is advisable to indicate to students that this be done carefully so that the shape of the pitcher is not altered.

I. The spout is pulled out slightly from the clay slab and, with the fingers, formed into the desired shape. Again, care must be taken not to distort the shape of the pitcher.

J. Students then reexamine the vase by Exekias. Specifically, they review the way the scene painted on it has been designed to complement the shape of the vase.

K. On sketch paper, students complete a number of designs which also seek to reflect and complement the shape of their pitchers. The best of these designs will take into account the contour lines of the handle.

# LESSON 6–3 (Continued)

L. When the pitcher is leather-hard, the entire surface is coated with a slip or engobe of a different color than the clay used to make the pitcher. (For example, a light-colored engobe might be applied to a pitcher made from a dark-colored clay.)

M. When the engobe is firm but still soft, the design is scratched or cut through, revealing the color of the contrasting clay body beneath. Various incising tools should be used to secure a variety of contrasting lines.

N. When completely dry, the vase is bisque fired.

VII. EVALUATION OF THE LESSON:
  A. RESPONSE:
  Did students use *formalism* as a guide to the *visual qualities* when examining an *ancient Greek* vase by *Exekias*? Were they able to explain how the scene on the vase is designed to complement the shape of the vessel? Did they point to the way the figures lean forward and the manner in which the lines of their backs curve to repeat the curve of the vase? Could they point out how the lines of the handles lead the viewer's eye to the center of the composition?

  B. PRODUCTION:
  Were students successful in completing a *clay slab pitcher* with a handle and a spout? Was the pitcher decorated with a sgraffito *line* pattern consisting of a *variety* of thick and thin lines? Did the sgraffito design complement the *form* of the pitcher?

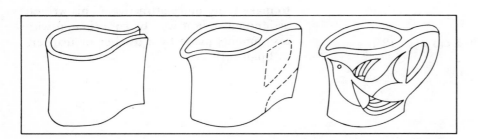

**Figure 9.**

I. TITLE OF THE LESSON: Drawing Exterior Views of Buildings—As They are

II. DURING THIS LESSON STUDENTS ARE TO ACQUIRE INFORMATION ABOUT THE FOLLOWING:

# LESSON 7–1

| RESPONSE | | | | PRODUCTION | | | | |
|---|---|---|---|---|---|---|---|---|
| Artists or Art Objects | Period or Style | Theories of Art | Aesthetic Qualities | Subject Matter | Elements of Art | Principles of Art | Media | Techniques |
| Examples of Roman Architecture | Roman Style of Architecture | | | Buildings, Areas in Need of Improvement | | | Pencil | Drawing |

III. OBJECTIVES:

A. RESPONSE:
Students will point out and name such important *architectural* features as columns, arches, keystones, barrel vaults, groin vaults, terraces, and domes observed in *Roman arches, temples, amphitheaters,* and *baths.* (Terms defined in text Glossary.)

B. PRODUCTION:
Students will complete three *pencil* drawings showing different exterior views of *buildings in the community judged to be in need of improvement.* Their *drawing* techniques will focus on accuracy and detail.

IV. VISUALS:
Temple of Fortuna Virilis (Figure 7.1)
Reconstructed model of the Sanctuary of Fortuna Primigenia (Figure 7.2)
Roman aqueduct in Segovia, Spain (Figures 7.4 and 7.7)
Central hall of the Baths of Caracalla (restoration drawing) (Figure 7.9)
Colosseum (Figures 7.10, 7.11, and 7.12)
Pantheon (Figure 7.13)
Arch of Constantine (Figure 7.17)

V. MATERIALS AND TOOLS NEEDED FOR THIS LESSON:
Pencils
White drawing paper (23 × 30.5 cm [9 × 12″])
Drawing boards

VI. PRESENTATION OF THE LESSON:

A. During a discussion of Roman architectural accomplishments, students examine and point out such features as columns, arches, keystones, barrel vaults, groin vaults, terraces, and domes observed in triumphal arches, temples, amphitheaters, and baths.

B. It is noted that the Romans were constantly building and rebuilding their cities to make them more attractive and impressive.

C. Emulating ancient Roman builders, each student is asked to search the community for a building in need of improvement. (This could be an individual or a team assignment.)

D. Students are then required to complete three accurate and detailed pencil drawings showing the building selected, each from a different point of view.

E. The completed drawing assignments are brought to class, displayed, and discussed. Suggestions for improving the outward appearance of each are solicited.

F. Students prepare a written report in which they describe the buildings selected for improvement, pointing out their shortcomings and specifying the improvements required to make them more attractive. (This written assignment might well be coordinated with assignments made by a teacher or teachers in English.)

## VII. EVALUATION OF THE LESSON:

### A. RESPONSE:

Were students able to point out and name such *architectural* features as columns, arches, keystones, barrel vaults, groin vaults, terraces, and domes found in *Roman arches, temples, amphitheaters,* and *baths?*

### B. PRODUCTION:

Did students complete three *pencil* drawings showing different exterior views of *buildings in the community judged to be in need of improvement?* Did their *drawing* techniques focus on accuracy and detail?

I. TITLE OF THE LESSON: Drawing Exterior
Views of Buildings—As They Could Be

II. DURING THIS LESSON STUDENTS ARE
TO ACQUIRE INFORMATION ABOUT THE
FOLLOWING:

# LESSON 7–2

| RESPONSE | | | | PRODUCTION | | | | |
|---|---|---|---|---|---|---|---|---|
| Artists or Art Objects | Period or Style | Theories of Art | Aesthetic Qualities | Subject Matter | Elements of Art | Principles of Art | Media | Techniques |
| Roman Monuments and Public Buildings | Roman Style of Architecture | | | | Value (Non-Color) | Emphasis<br><br>Gradation | Pencil | Drawing |

III. OBJECTIVES:

A. RESPONSE:

Students recognize that ancient *Roman monuments* and *public buildings* were numerous and impressive. They are able to identify structures such as baths, circuses, triumphal arches, forums, aqueducts, temples, and amphitheaters and understand that these were constructed for the enjoyment of the people and to maintain the popularity of the emperors.

B. PRODUCTION:

Referring to the suggestions made in the written report prepared for the previous lesson (Lesson 7–1), students are to *draw* with *pencil* the same building as it would appear if all their recommendations for improvement were implemented. The three-dimensional aspects of the objects included in their drawings will be *emphasized* by the use of *value* contrast and *gradation*.

IV. VISUALS:

Temple of Fortuna Virilis (Figure 7.1)
Reconstructed model of the Sanctuary of Fortuna Primigenia (Figure 7.2)
Roman aqueduct in Segovia, Spain (Figures 7.4 and 7.7)
Central hall of the Baths of Caracalla (restoration drawing) (Figure 7.9)
Colosseum (Figures 7.10, 7.11, and 7.12)
Pantheon (Figure 7.13)
Arch of Constantine (Figure 7.17)
Arch of Bara (Figure 7.18)

V. MATERIALS AND TOOLS NEEDED FOR THIS LESSON:

Pencils
White drawing paper (23 × 30.5 cm [9 × 12″])

VI. PRESENTATION OF THE LESSON:

A. Students reexamine a number of Roman monuments and public buildings, discussing their appearances, functions, and the reasons why they were built.

B. The written reports prepared for the previous lesson (Lesson 7–1) are discussed. Each student (or team of students if a team approach is used) will describe in detail what they would do to improve upon the outward appearance of the building they selected.

C. Students are then asked to complete a detailed pencil drawing showing the building as it would appear if all their suggestions for improvement were implemented. In these drawings, attention will be directed to using value contrast and gradation to emphasize the three-dimensional aspects of the objects illustrated.

D. A display consisting of the written report, and "before" and "after" drawings would be planned and set up by each student (or student team).

## VII. EVALUATION OF THE LESSON:

### A. RESPONSE:
Were students able to identify such *Roman monuments* and *public buildings* as baths, circuses, triumphal arches, forums, aqueducts, temples, and amphitheaters? Could they explain the functions of these structures and provide reasons why they were built?

### B. PRODUCTION:
Did student *pencil drawings* incorporate the suggestions for improvement indicated in their written reports? Were the three-dimensional aspects of the objects included in their drawings *emphasized* by the use of *value* contrast and *gradation*?

I. TITLE OF THE LESSON: Making Ceramic Tesserae

II. DURING THIS LESSON STUDENTS ARE TO ACQUIRE INFORMATION ABOUT THE FOLLOWING:

# LESSON 8–1

| RESPONSE | | | | PRODUCTION | | | | |
|---|---|---|---|---|---|---|---|---|
| Artists or Art Objects | Period or Style | Theories of Art | Aesthetic Qualities | Subject Matter | Elements of Art | Principles of Art | Media | Techniques |
| Examples of Byzantine Mosaics | Byzantine | | Expressive Qualities | Ceramic Tesserae | Hue | | Clay Glaze | Slab Construction Glazing |

III. OBJECTIVES:
   A. RESPONSE:
   Students learn that brilliantly colored mosaics were often used as interior decorations in *Byzantine* churches. They also realize that these mosaics were meant to appeal to the emotions. By referring to their *expressive qualities,* students gain insights into the meanings and feelings generated in viewers by Byzantine church mosaics.

   B. PRODUCTION:
   Students make *ceramic tesserae* from 0.6-cm [¼-inch] thick *clay slabs* which are *glazed,* cut into small (approximately 1.3 cm [½″]) square and rectangular shapes, and fired. Not less than five *hues* of tesserae will be produced by each student.

IV. VISUALS:
   Apse decorations from Sant' Apollinare in Classe (Figure 8.5)
   *The Virgin and Child with the Emperors Justinian and Constantine* (Figure 8.10)
   *Justinian and Attendants* (Figure 8.12)
   *Theodora and Attendants* (Figure 8.13)

V. MATERIALS AND TOOLS NEEDED FOR THIS LESSON:
   Pencils
   Newsprint
   Colored pencils, crayons, or tempera paint
   Water-base clay
   Wood slats (0.6-cm [¼-inch] thick)
   Rolling pins
   Fettling knives
   Colored glazes
   Brushes (for glaze application)
   Pieces of cloth, burlap, or canvas

VI. PRESENTATION OF THE LESSON:
   A. Students examine examples of mosaics used as interior decorations in Sant' Apollinare in Classe, Hagia Sophia, and San Vitale. A consideration of their literal qualities leads to a discussion of the moods, feelings, and ideas generated by these mosaics. Attention is then directed to the way these colorful surface decorations were made, that is, by arranging small pieces of glazed clay called "tesserae" into a design.

   B. Students are instructed to complete several 30.5 × 30.5-cm [12 × 12-inch] pencil sketches showing various designs for mosaics.

   C. A color scheme consisting of no less than five hues is applied to the best of the designs. Crayons, colored pencils, or tempera paints may be used for this purpose.

   D. The design is then divided into small sections to determine the number of tesserae needed to make it. The sections should be small—about 1.3 cm [½″] square—and can be of uniform or varied shapes.

   E. Each student then prepares a clay slab for every color used in his or her design. These slabs are rolled out between 0.6-cm [¼-inch] thick wood slats. Rounded edges are trimmed off when the clay slabs are leather-hard.

   F. Glazes are brushed liberally over the damp clay slabs. Students are instructed to apply several coats of glaze at right angles to each other when the shine leaves the surface. At least three coats are applied in this manner.

G. When the glazed slabs are firm but not dry, they are cut into small shapes with a fettling knife. Cuts are made straight down rather than at an angle. Typical shapes are square or rectangular, although other shapes may be made if students choose to do so. However, the shapes should not be large—1.3 cm [½″] is customary.

H. Allow the tesserae to dry slowly to prevent warping. They are then placed on kiln shelves and fired.

## VII. EVALUATION OF THE LESSON:

A. RESPONSE:

Were students aware that mosaics were often used as interior decorations in *Byzantine* churches? Did they refer to *expressive qualities* when attempting to gain insights into the meanings and feelings generated by Byzantine mosaics?

B. PRODUCTION:

Did students produce *glazed ceramic tesserae* from 0.6-cm [¼-inch] thick *clay slabs*? Did each student's collection of tesserae reveal at least *five* different hues?

I. TITLE OF THE LESSON: Using Ceramic Tesserae to Make Mosaic Wall Plaques

II. DURING THIS LESSON STUDENTS ARE TO ACQUIRE INFORMATION ABOUT THE FOLLOWING:

# LESSON 8–2

| RESPONSE | | | | PRODUCTION | | | | |
|---|---|---|---|---|---|---|---|---|
| Artists or Art Objects | Period or Style | Theories of Art | Aesthetic Qualities | Subject Matter | Elements of Art | Principles of Art | Media | Techniques |
| Examples of Byzantine Mosaics | Byzantine | | | Wall Plaque | Hue | | Ceramic Tesserae | Mosaic |

III. OBJECTIVES:

A. RESPONSE:

Students learn that *Byzantine* artists chose to decorate their church interiors with mosaics because they were brilliantly colored and could be seen from great distances.

B. PRODUCTION:

Using the glazed *ceramic tesserae* made in the previous lesson (Lesson 8–1), students complete a 30.5 × 30.5-cm [12 × 12-inch] *mosaic wall plaque*. Tesserae will be cemented neatly and precisely and the narrow openings between them filled with grout (defined in text Glossary). A minimum of five *hues* will be used in each mosaic.

IV. VISUALS:

Apse decorations from Sant' Apollinare in Classe (Figure 8.5)

*The Virgin and Child with the Emperors Justinian and Constantine* (Figure 8.10)

*Justinian and Attendants* (Figure 8.12)

*Theodora and Attendants* (Figure 8.13)

V. MATERIALS AND TOOLS NEEDED FOR THIS LESSON:

Ceramic tesserae

Waterproofed backing of 1.5-cm [⅝-inch] marine plywood or 1.3-cm [½-inch] tempered hardboard (30.5 × 30.5 cm [12 × 12″])

Household cement (note any precautions on label and see Safety Note in text, page 242)

Grout

Sponge

Pieces of cloth

VI. PRESENTATION OF THE LESSON:

A. Students again examine examples of mosaics from Sant' Apollinare in Classe, Hagia Sophia, and San Vitale, noting their brilliant colors which produced a dream-like setting. Attention is also directed to the precision with which Byzantine artists arranged the tesserae in their compositions.

B. Mosaic designs completed in the previous lesson (Lesson 8–1) are transferred to sturdy, waterproofed backings such as 1.5-cm [⅝-inch] marine plywood or the rough side of 1.3-cm [½-inch] tempered hardboard.

C. Any household cement can be used to attach the tesserae to the backings. Students are told to coat each tessera with cement and press it in place with a slight twist.

D. Circular designs should be started at the center. Tesserae should not touch. If crowded, they may buckle as the cement dries. Work should be kept clean—excess cement should be wiped off as each section of the design is completed.

E. The plaque is grouted when all the tesserae are cemented in place. Tesserae are first moistened with water and the grout, mixed to a creamy paste, is rubbed into the grooves between them. The grout is allowed to set a few minutes, and then the excess is sponged off. (Grout can be tinted with tempera paint if desired.) To prevent cracking and powdering, it is advisable to cure the grouted mosaics for three days under wet cloths. (See Safety Note in text, page 136.)

## VII. EVALUATION OF THE LESSON:

### A. RESPONSE:

Did students learn that *Byzantine* artists decorated their church interiors with mosaics because they were brilliantly colored and could be seen from great distances?

### B. PRODUCTION:

Did students complete a 30.5 × 30.5-cm [12 × 12-inch] *mosaic wall plaque* with the glazed *ceramic tesserae* made in the previous lesson? Were the tesserae cemented neatly and precisely? Were the narrow openings or grooves between the tesserae filled with grout? Did students use at least five *hues* in their mosaics?

**Mosaic design (secondary-level student work)**

I. TITLE OF THE LESSON: Crayon Etching in the Style of Romanesque Manuscript Illustrations

II. DURING THIS LESSON STUDENTS ARE TO ACQUIRE INFORMATION ABOUT THE FOLLOWING:

# LESSON 9–1

| RESPONSE | | | | PRODUCTION | | | | |
|---|---|---|---|---|---|---|---|---|
| Artists or Art Objects | Period or Style | Theories of Art | Aesthetic Qualities | Subject Matter | Elements of Art | Principles of Art | Media | Techniques |
| Medieval Manuscript Illustrations | Early Medieval<br><br>Romanesque | Formalism | Visual Qualities | | Intensity<br>Shape<br>Line<br>Texture (Simulated) | Balance (Asymmetrical)<br>Variety<br>Harmony | Crayon<br><br>India Ink | "Etching" |

III. OBJECTIVES:

A. RESPONSE:

Drawing upon their knowledge of the *visual qualities* stressed by *formalism,* students are able to point out the distinctive combinations of elements and principles that characterized the art of the *Early Medieval* and *Romanesque* periods. Focusing on two Medieval manuscript illustrations, they will note the variety of contrasting lines in one *(St. Matthew)* and the flat, intensely colored shapes in another *(Annunciation).*

B. PRODUCTION:

Students will complete a *crayon etching* composed of *intensely colored, flat shapes;* a *variety* of contrasting thick and thin *lines;* and an overall *simulated texture.* Texture will be achieved by scratching through an *inked* coating to a *crayoned* surface. Three textures will be repeated throughout the *asymmetrically balanced* composition to assure *harmony.*

IV. VISUALS:

*St. Matthew,* from the *Gospel Book of Archbishop Ebbo of Reims* (Figure 9.6)
*Annunciation,* from a Swabian Gospel Manuscript (Figure 9.24)

V. MATERIALS AND TOOLS NEEDED FOR THIS LESSON:

Pencils
Newsprint
Newspaper (with which to cover desks or tables)
White drawing paper (23 × 30.5 cm [9 × 12″])
Crayons
India ink
Brushes
Pointed instruments used to scratch, or "etch," a textured pattern (nails, scissors, compass point, etc.)

VI. PRESENTATION OF THE LESSON:

A. The two Medieval manuscript illustrations are studied. Discussion centers on the bold use of contrasting lines in the *St. Matthew* and the flat, intensely colored shapes in the *Annunciation.* In answer to teacher-posed questions, students observe that the figures in both illustrations appear to be speaking or listening.

B. Students are asked to produce several sketches which show two people engaged in a spirited conversation. One of the figures should be made to look as though it is speaking while the other is intently listening.

C. The completed sketches are exhibited and discussed. The teacher then asks students to select their most successful sketches and reproduce them in pencil on white drawing paper. They are told to eliminate details and simplify shapes in these drawings.

D. Students are next told to go over the pencil lines in their drawings with India ink. These ink lines are applied with a fine brush.

Students are advised to vary the pressure on the brush to produce a variety of contrasting lines.

E. The drawings are colored with a heavy application of crayon. The entire composition is crayoned with light, intense colors.

F. A coating of India ink is brushed thoroughly over each of the crayon drawings. The ink will adhere to the crayon surface more easily if a chalk eraser is first patted lightly over the entire drawing.

G. While the ink is drying, students are instructed to design a textured pattern to be etched on their compositions. Three different textures must be repeated in each work to enhance overall harmony. For example, one student may decide to divide his or her work into six square sections with a ruler and use a combination of fine lines to create different textured surfaces in each section. However, no more than three different textures should be used throughout the composition.*

H. The pattern is scratched in the surface of the inked drawing with a pointed instrument. This brings out the brightly colored shapes and contrasting lines of the original drawing. (Safety Note: Extra caution should always be exercised when sharp or pointed instruments are used.)

---

*If the principle of *variety* were to be stressed, a greater number of different *textures* would be called for.

# LESSON 9–1 (Continued)

VII. EVALUATION OF THE LESSON:

A. RESPONSE:
Did students refer to the *visual qualities* stressed by *formalism* when pointing out the distinctive combinations of elements and principles that characterize *Early Medieval* and *Romanesque* art? Did they note the variety of contrasting lines in one Medieval manuscript *(St. Matthew)* and the flat, intensely colored shapes in another *(Annunciation)?*

B. PRODUCTION:
Did students complete a *crayon etching* composed of *intensely colored, flat shapes;* a *variety* of contrasting thick and thin *lines;* and an overall *simulated texture?* Was the textured surface achieved by scratching through an *inked* coating to a *crayoned* surface? Were three textures repeated throughout *asymmetrically balanced* compositions to assure *harmony?*

I. TITLE OF THE LESSON: Woodblock Prints of Fantastic Creatures

II. DURING THIS LESSON STUDENTS ARE TO ACQUIRE INFORMATION ABOUT THE FOLLOWING:

# LESSON 9–2

| RESPONSE | | | | PRODUCTION | | | | |
|---|---|---|---|---|---|---|---|---|
| Artists or Art Objects | Period or Style | Theories of Art | Aesthetic Qualities | Subject Matter | Elements of Art | Principles of Art | Media | Techniques |
| Examples of Romanesque Carving | Romanesque | Emotionalism | Expressive Qualities | Imaginary Creatures | Space (Positive and Negative) | | Wood Block | Printmaking |

III. OBJECTIVES:
   A. RESPONSE:
   Examining examples of *Romanesque carving*, students learn that Medieval artists often included fantastic, imaginary creatures in their carvings and manuscript illustrations. They refer to the *expressive qualities* stressed by *emotionalism* when they try to determine the possible meanings for these unusual creatures.

   B. PRODUCTION:
   Students complete a *woodblock print* of an *imaginary creature* that is as fanciful as possible. They learn to distinguish between *positive* and *negative space* and demonstrate this by carving away the negative spaces in the creature designs they have transferred to blocks of wood. They demonstrate a concern for neatness when inking and *printing* these carved wood blocks.

IV. VISUALS:
   Relief carving, Santes Creus Monastery (Figure 9.21)
   Capital carving, cloister of the Cathedral at Tarragona (Figure 9.22)

V. MATERIALS AND TOOLS NEEDED FOR THIS LESSON:
   Pencils
   Newsprint
   Carbon paper
   Pieces of soft pine wood (approximately 20.3 × 25.4 cm [8 × 10″])
   Carving tools (V- or U-shaped gouges with wooden handles)
   Water-soluble printer's ink
   Brayers

Ink slab (A food tray or a 25.4 × 25.4 cm [10 × 10″] piece of glass with taped edges to prevent cutting can be used for this purpose.)
Newspapers
Paper (white drawing paper and/or colored construction paper)

VI. PRESENTATION OF THE LESSON:
   A. Students examine and discuss the examples of Romanesque carving, paying particular attention to the expressive qualities in each. The discussion focuses upon the fantastic creatures often found in Medieval works of art. Students are encouraged to express their opinions about why these unusual creatures may have been created.
   B. Using pencil and newsprint, and giving full reign to their imaginations, students design their own fantastic creatures. These sketches are done on pieces of paper that are cut to the same size as the wood blocks on which they will be working.
   C. Using a sharp pencil and carbon paper, students transfer their most successful designs to the wood blocks. They then identify the positive and negative spaces in their designs and carve away all the negative spaces. They are reminded that the negative spaces that have been carved away will not be printed.
   D. Students are instructed to make all cuts in the direction of the wood grain while carving. Cuts made across the grain will bind the carving tool and may splinter the wood.

They are also cautioned to make certain that the hand holding the wood block is always kept away from the path of the carving tool.* (This Safety Note is also included in the text, page 159.)

E. The design can be checked from time to time by placing a piece of newsprint on the carving and rubbing over the surface with the side of a pencil.

F. When the carving has been completed, a small amount of printer's ink is squeezed from the tube onto an ink slab.

G. The ink is then rolled with a brayer until it is spread thoroughly over the ink slab.

H. The brayer is applied to the carved wood block until it is completely and evenly covered.

I. Students may choose from two printing methods:

1. The inked block is carefully placed face-down on a sheet of white drawing paper (or colored construction paper) and pressed down firmly by hand. Several thicknesses of newspaper placed under the paper on which the printing is done will result in a better-quality print.

2. A sheet of white drawing paper (or colored construction paper) is placed over the inked wood block and rubbed firmly with the fingers or a large spoon. Before removing the paper, it is advisable to pull back a corner to determine if additional rubbing is called for.

J. For additional prints, students are instructed to re-ink their wood blocks.

---

*Easily constructed wooden bench hooks are ideal for use during the cutting operations required in printmaking. Hooked over the edge of a desk or table, they hold the wood blocks in place and make cutting less hazardous for students (Figure 10).

# LESSON 9–2 (Continued)

VII. EVALUATION OF THE LESSON:

A. RESPONSE:

After examining examples of *Romanesque carving,* did students acknowledge that Medieval artists often included fantastic, imaginary creatures in their artworks? Did they refer to the *expressive qualities* stressed by *emotionalism* when trying to determine the possible meanings for these unusual creatures?

B. PRODUCTION:

Did students complete a *woodblock* print of an *imaginary creature?* Could they successfully distinguish between the *positive* and *negative spaces* in their creature designs? Did they demonstrate this by carving away the negative spaces in their creature designs once they had been transferred to blocks of wood? Did their finished prints show that they exercised neatness during the *printing* process?

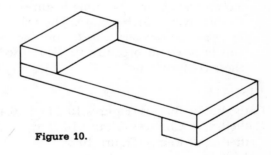

**Figure 10.**

I. TITLE OF THE LESSON: String Print of a Gothic Cathedral

II. DURING THIS LESSON STUDENTS ARE TO ACQUIRE INFORMATION ABOUT THE FOLLOWING:

# LESSON 10–1

| RESPONSE | | | | PRODUCTION | | | | |
|---|---|---|---|---|---|---|---|---|
| Artists or Art Objects | Period or Style | Theories of Art | Aesthetic Qualities | Subject Matter | Elements of Art | Principles of Art | Media | Techniques |
| Examples of Gothic Cathedrals | Gothic | | | Church Façade | Line | Emphasis Harmony Variety Movement | String | Printmaking |

III. OBJECTIVES:
   A. RESPONSE:
      Students are able to identify the principal features that characterize the *Gothic style* of architecture. When examining several examples of *Gothic cathedrals,* they can successfully point out such features as the following: a bold vertical emphasis; large central portals; rose windows; tall, pointed spires; flying buttresses; tympana; pointed arches; and piers. (Terms defined in text Glossary.)
   B. PRODUCTION:
      Students will complete a large *string print* of a *church façade* incorporating features of the Gothic style of architecture. The principles of *emphasis, harmony, variety,* and *movement* will be used to organize the *lines* used in these compositions.

IV. VISUALS:
   Cathedral of Burgos (Figures 10.2 and 10.4)
   Cathedral of Chartres (Figure 10.7)
   Cathedral of Reims (Figure 10.8)

V. MATERIALS AND TOOLS NEEDED FOR THIS LESSON:
   Pencils
   Newsprint
   Pieces of cardboard cut from corrugated boxes (about 30.5 × 46 cm [12 × 18"])
   Heavy string or cord
   Newspapers (with which to cover desks or tables)
   Water-soluble printer's ink
   White drawing paper (30.5 × 46 cm [12 × 18"])
   Glue (see Safety Note in text, page 242)
   Brayers

VI. PRESENTATION OF THE LESSON:
   A. During a discussion of the Gothic cathedrals at Burgos, Chartres, and Reims, students are asked to identify and point to the main features of this architectural style. Particular attention is directed to the obvious vertical movement or rhythm noted in these structures.
   B. On newsprint, students complete several line drawings of cathedral façades. They are asked to capture the same vertical, soaring emphasis observed in the Gothic cathedrals they have studied. This can be done by making the vertical lines longer and more numerous so that they dominate in the composition.
   C. In addition, student drawings must also contain the following:
      1. A central portal and two side portals with one or more tympana.
      2. A large, elaborate rose window.
      3. No less than eight other windows with pointed arches.
      4. A minimum of two tall, richly decorated pointed towers or spires.
   D. Some students may opt to include flying buttresses in their compositions as well.
   E. The most successful of their line drawings is reproduced on a large piece of corrugated cardboard cut from an ordinary box. This piece of cardboard should measure about 30.5 × 46 cm [12 × 18"].

F. Lengths of heavy string or cord are cut and glued in place over the lines in the drawing. A complex pattern of contrasting, repetitious lines is sought.

G. A water-soluble printing ink is rolled over the cardboard-and-cord composition with a brayer. (Refer to printing instructions provided in Lesson 9–2.)

H. A sheet of white drawing paper is placed over the inked composition and rubbed firmly with the fingers or a spoon to produce a print. A clean brayer may also be used for this purpose.

I. Subsequent prints made by re-inking the cardboard-and-string compositions are usually more successful than is the first print produced with this method.

VII. EVALUATION OF THE LESSON:

A. RESPONSE:
Were students able to identify the features that characterize the *Gothic style* of architecture? When examining several examples of *Gothic cathedrals*, could they point out such features as the following: a bold vertical emphasis; large central portals; rose windows; tall, pointed spires; flying buttresses; tympana; pointed arches; and piers?

B. PRODUCTION:
Did students complete a large *string print* of a *church façade* which incorporated features of the Gothic style of architecture? Were the principles of *emphasis, harmony, variety,* and *movement* used to organize the *lines* used in these compositions?

I. TITLE OF THE LESSON: Drawing Personal Tympana

II. DURING THIS LESSON STUDENTS ARE TO ACQUIRE INFORMATION ABOUT THE FOLLOWING:

# LESSON 10–2

| RESPONSE | | | | PRODUCTION | | | | |
|---|---|---|---|---|---|---|---|---|
| **Artists or Art Objects** | **Period or Style** | **Theories of Art** | **Aesthetic Qualities** | **Subject Matter** | **Elements of Art** | **Principles of Art** | **Media** | **Techniques** |
| Examples of Romanesque and Gothic Tympana | Romanesque and Early Gothic Later Gothic | Imitationalism Formalism Emotionalism | Literal Visual Expressive | | Shape | Balance (Symmetrical, Asymmetrical) | Pencil | Drawing |

III. OBJECTIVES:

A. RESPONSE:

While examining several *Romanesque* and *Gothic tympana,* students refer to the *literal qualities* stressed by *imitationalism* to ascertain the growing Gothic concern for realism. They also focus on the *visual qualities* emphasized by *formalism* to determine that the *Romanesque and early Gothic* tympana were usually symmetrically balanced. *Later Gothic* tympana make use of a more natural asymmetrical balance. Concentrating on the *expressive qualities* favored by *emotionalism,* students observe that Gothic art exhibited a new awareness for human emotions. They are able to point this out especially in the tympanum from the Cathedral of Pamplona.

B. PRODUCTION:

Students complete a *pencil drawing* of specified subject matter in which all the *shapes* are designed to fit within a half-round or triangular shape that measures no less than 30.5 cm [12″] in length and 20 cm [8″] in height. Half the class will *balance* the shapes in their drawings *symmetrically.* The other half of the class will balance the shapes in their drawings *asymmetrically.*

IV. VISUALS:

West portal, Leyre Monastery (Figure 9.17)

Tympanum, Santa Maria, Sangüesa (Figure 9.18)

Sarmental portal, Cathedral of Burgos (Figure 10.12)

*Death of the Virgin,* Cathedral of Pamplona (Figure 10.13)

V. MATERIALS AND TOOLS NEEDED FOR THIS LESSON:

Pencils

Newsprint

VI. PRESENTATION OF THE LESSON:

A. Students compare and contrast examples of Romanesque and Gothic tympana. They observe the increased concern for realism evident in Gothic tympana. They also note how the figures and objects in Romanesque and early Gothic tympana are balanced symmetrically, while figures and objects in later Gothic tympana are balanced asymmetrically. Discussion also covers the Gothic concern for human emotions, a concern that is not as pronounced in the earlier Romanesque tympana.

B. Students are asked to complete several preliminary sketches that show themselves involved in various school-related activities. They might choose to show themselves at a school dance, participating or viewing a sporting event, or studying in the library. While other figures and objects are to be included in these sketches, each student is to make certain that his or her own figure dominates as the center of attention.

C. Students next select what they regard as their most interesting sketches. They are told to redesign these sketches to fit comfortably within a half-round or triangular shape measuring no less than 30.5 cm [12"] in length and 20 cm [8"] in height. These half-round or triangular shapes are to be cut from large sheets of newsprint.

D. One half of the class is instructed to balance the shapes in their drawings symmetrically, while the other half of the class must balance the shapes in their drawings asymmetrically.

## VII. EVALUATION OF THE LESSON:

A. RESPONSE:

Did students focus on the *literal qualities* stressed by *imitationalism* to note the increased concern for reality when comparing *Gothic tympana* to *Romanesque tympana?* Did they refer to the *visual qualities* emphasized by *formalism* to determine that *Romanesque and early Gothic* tympana were symmetrically balanced while *later Gothic* tympana were asymmetrically balanced? Concentrating on the *expressive qualities* favored by *emotionalism,* were students able to perceive the growing concern for human emotions evident in Gothic tympana, especially the tympanum from the Cathedral of Pamplona?

B. PRODUCTION:

Did students complete a *pencil drawing* of specified subject matter in which all the *shapes* were designed to fit within a half-round or triangular shape that measured no less than 30.5 cm [12"] in length and 20 cm [8"] in height? Were the drawings completed by one half of the class *balanced symmetrically?* Were the drawings of the remaining half of the class balanced *asymmetrically?*

I. TITLE OF THE LESSON: Carving Personal Tympanum Reliefs in Clay

II. DURING THIS LESSON STUDENTS ARE TO ACQUIRE INFORMATION ABOUT THE FOLLOWING:

# LESSON 10-3

| RESPONSE | | | | PRODUCTION | | | | |
|---|---|---|---|---|---|---|---|---|
| Artists or Art Objects | Period or Style | Theories of Art | Aesthetic Qualities | Subject Matter | Elements of Art | Principles of Art | Media | Techniques |
| Examples of Gothic Tympana | Gothic | Emotionalism | Expressive Qualities | | Shape Texture (Actual) Value (Non-Color) | Balance (Symmetrical, Asymmetrical) Variety | Clay | Relief Carving |

III. OBJECTIVES:

A. RESPONSE:

Focusing on the *expressive qualities* emphasized by *emotionalism,* students learn that the people depicted in *Gothic tympana* carvings were no longer mere symbols for religious figures. Rather, they are presented as real people expressing genuine human emotions.

B. PRODUCTION:

Students complete *clay relief carvings* exhibiting a *variety* of six *contrasting textures.* Specified subject matter is designed to fit within half-round or triangular *shapes* that measure no less than 30.5 cm [12″] in length and 20 cm [8″] in height. Half the class will *balance* the shapes in their reliefs *symmetrically.* The other half of the class will balance the shapes in their reliefs *asymmetrically.* A variety of light and dark *values* will be used to create an interesting surface pattern.

IV. VISUALS:

Sarmental portal, Cathedral of Burgos (Figure 10.12)

*Death of the Virgin,* Cathedral of Pamplona (Figure 10.13)

V. MATERIALS AND TOOLS NEEDED FOR THIS LESSON:

Tympanum drawings from the previous lesson (Lesson 10-2)
Water-base clay
Wood slats (2.54-cm [1-inch] thick)
Rolling pins
Clay-modeling tools
Pieces of cloth, burlap, or canvas
*Optional Materials:*
  Colored glazes
  Brushes (for glaze application)
  Powdered tempera paint (black, blue-green, and green)
  Paste wax
  Polishing cloths

VI. PRESENTATION OF THE LESSON:

A. Students again examine the tympanum carvings from the cathedrals of Burgos and Pamplona and observe how the figures depicted in these Gothic works exhibit, by their expressions and gestures, genuine human emotions.

B. Continued discussion centers on the high relief and textural variety noted in both artworks. This discussion terminates with a brief review of the previous lesson (Lesson 10-2), during which students again note the following:

1. The way figures and objects in the tympana are organized to fit within a specified shape.

2. The use of symmetrical balance in the Burgos tympanum and asymmetrical balance in the Pamplona tympanum.

C. Students then roll out large slabs of clay to a uniform 2.54-cm [1-inch] thickness, using wood slats and rolling pins. These slabs must be large enough to accommodate the 30.5 × 20-cm [12 × 8-inch] tympanum designs completed in the previous lesson. Students place these designs directly on the clay slabs and trace over the lines with a sharp pencil. In this manner, the designs are transferred to the clay slab.

D. With clay-modeling tools, students "carve" out their pictures in the soft clay. No modeling techniques are employed in this instance. Instead, students use a subtractive technique to create a panel in high relief characterized by contrasting light and dark (shadowed) areas.

E. Students are also told to include no less than six contrasting textured surfaces in their reliefs.

F. Finished reliefs are bisque fired and, if desired, glazed. However, some students may opt to give their reliefs a bronze-like patina.* This is done by mixing black powdered tempera paint with a paste wax and rubbing this over the entire surface of the relief with a cloth. A second mixture of green or blue-green powdered tempera and paste wax is applied lightly over the blackened surface so that the raised portions of the carving will be highlighted. Finally, the relief is polished lightly with a clean, soft cloth. (See Safety Note in text, page 180.)

# LESSON 10–3 (Continued)

VII. EVALUATION OF THE LESSON:
  A. RESPONSE:
    Did students focus on the *expressive qualities* emphasized by *emotionalism* to learn that the people depicted in *Gothic tympana* carvings were no longer mere symbols for religious figures? Did they recognize that Gothic artists were attempting to represent real people expressing genuine human emotions?

  B. PRODUCTION:
    Did the completed *clay relief carvings* exhibit a *variety* of six *contrasting textures*? Were students successful in designing the specified subject matter to fit within half-round or triangular *shapes* measuring no less than 30.5 cm [12″] in length and 20 cm [8″] in height? Did one half the class *balance* the shapes in their reliefs *symmetrically*? Did the other half of the class balance the shapes in their reliefs *asymmetrically*? Did the reliefs reveal a variety of light and dark values to create an interesting surface pattern?

---

*Patina* is defined as a film which can form naturally on bronze and copper (by long exposure to air) or artificially (as by the application of acid, paint, etc.) to a surface.

---

*Another simulated bronze patina can be achieved by using shellac (white or orange) and powdered tempera paint in the following manner:

1. Generous portions of black, green, and blue-green powdered tempera paint are poured from their containers onto sheets of newspaper spread over a table top in a large, well-ventilated room.
2. A *small* amount of shellac is poured into a flat container. The amount is kept small since the unused shellac will be too contaminated for future use.
3. A stiff brush is dipped into the shellac and then into the black powdered tempera paint. This mixture is brushed thoroughly over the entire relief, including the edges.
4. When the entire surface of the relief is blackened and while it is still tacky, a light application of green or blue-green powdered tempera is brushed over the entire surface. In this way, the raised portions of the relief will be highlighted.
5. The "patina" process can be repeated on any section of the relief that fails to look bronze-like.
6. Before considering this patina technique, read the section entitled "Safety in the Art Studio" on pages 110-111 of this *Teacher's Resource Book.*

I. TITLE OF THE LESSON: Painting a Landscape with Gradations of Value to Emphasize Space*

II. DURING THIS LESSON STUDENTS ARE TO ACQUIRE INFORMATION ABOUT THE FOLLOWING:

# LESSON 11–1

| RESPONSE | | | | PRODUCTION | | | | |
|---|---|---|---|---|---|---|---|---|
| Artists or Art Objects | Period or Style | Theories of Art | Aesthetic Qualities | Subject Matter | Elements of Art | Principles of Art | Media | Techniques |
| Masaccio Botticelli Raphael | Renaissance | Formalism | Visual Qualities | Landscape | Value (Color) Shape Space | Emphasis Gradation Variety | Tempera Paint | Painting |

III. OBJECTIVES:
   A. RESPONSE:
   While considering the *visual qualities* stressed by *formalism,* students observe that *Renaissance* artists such as *Masaccio, Botticelli,* and *Raphael* were concerned with creating an illusion of depth or space in their paintings as a way of making them appear more life-like. They are able to define "aerial, or atmospheric, perspective" (terms defined in text Glossary) and can explain how value gradation can be used to help achieve the appearance of distance in a painting.

   B. PRODUCTION:
   Students complete a *landscape painting* in which all forms are shown as two-dimensional, overlapping *shapes.* These shapes are *painted* in a *variety* of *values* obtained by mixing white and black *tempera paints.* Values will be used to *emphasize* the element of *space.* Those used on the nearest objects depicted in this landscape will be dark. Values applied to objects in the distance will be *gradually* lighter. The lightest value will be used for the object or objects located furthest back in space.

IV. VISUALS:
   Masaccio, *The Tribute Money* (Figure 11.3)
   Botticelli, *The Adoration of the Magi* (Figure 11.14)
   Raphael, *The Alba Madonna* (Figure 11.21)

V. MATERIALS AND TOOLS NEEDED FOR THIS LESSON:
   Pencils
   White drawing paper (23 × 30.5 cm [9 × 12"])
   Tempera paint (black and white only)
   Brushes
   Paint cloths
   Mixing trays
   Water containers

VI. PRESENTATION OF THE LESSON:
   A. A discussion of several Renaissance paintings will include a consideration of aerial, or atmospheric, perspective. Students will note how objects furthest back in these paintings are painted in lighter, duller hues.
   B. Students are asked to compile an extensive list on the chalkboard of objects that might be included in a landscape painting. After this is done, each student selects at least eight items from this list and arranges these as two-dimensional, overlapping shapes in a landscape composition.
   C. The landscape compositions are then painted with a range of values secured by mixing white and black tempera paints. Dark values will be applied to objects in the foreground. Objects further back in the compositions will be painted in values that become gradually lighter and lighter. The lightest values are reserved for objects located furthest back in the composition.

---

*It is suggested that half the class complete this lesson focusing on value gradation to emphasize space, while the other half of the class completes the following lesson (Lesson 11–2), which focuses on intensity gradation to suggest space.

## VII. EVALUATION OF THE LESSON:

### A. RESPONSE:

Having considered the *visual qualities* stressed by *formalism,* did students acknowledge that *Renaissance* artists such as *Masaccio, Botticelli,* and *Raphael* were concerned with creating an illusion of depth in their paintings as a way of making them more lifelike? Could they define "aerial, or atmospheric, perspective"? Were they able to explain how value gradation can be used to help achieve the appearance of distance in a painting?

### B. PRODUCTION:

Did students complete a *landscape painting* in which all forms are shown as two-dimensional, overlapping *shapes*? Were the shapes in this landscape *painted* in a *variety* of *values* obtained by mixing white and black *tempera paints*? Were the values used to *emphasize* the element of *space*? Did the values become *gradually* lighter as students painted objects further and further back into space?

# LESSON 11–1 (Continued)

**Landscape (secondary-level student work)**

I. TITLE OF THE LESSON: Painting a Landscape with Gradations of Intensity to Emphasize Space*

II. DURING THIS LESSON STUDENTS ARE TO ACQUIRE INFORMATION ABOUT THE FOLLOWING:

# LESSON 11–2

| RESPONSE | | | | PRODUCTION | | | | |
|---|---|---|---|---|---|---|---|---|
| Artists or Art Objects | Period or Style | Theories of Art | Aesthetic Qualities | Subject Matter | Elements of Art | Principles of Art | Media | Techniques |
| Masaccio Botticelli Raphael | Renaissance | Formalism | Visual Qualities | Landscape | Intensity Shape Space | Emphasis Gradation Variety | Tempera Paint | Painting |

III. OBJECTIVES:

A. RESPONSE:

While considering the *visual qualities* stressed by *formalism*, students observe that *Renaissance* artists such as *Masaccio, Botticelli,* and *Raphael* were concerned with creating an illusion of depth or space in their paintings as a way of making them appear more lifelike. They are able to define "aerial, or atmospheric, perspective" and can explain how gradation in color intensity can be used to help achieve the appearance of distance in a painting.

B. PRODUCTION:

Students complete a *landscape painting* with *tempera paint* in which all forms are shown as two-dimensional, overlapping *shapes*. These shapes are painted in a *variety* of *intensities* obtained by mixing two complementary colors of the students' own choosing. Different intensities of the same hue are used to *emphasize* the element of *space*. Those used on the nearest objects depicted in this landscape will be bright. Intensities applied to objects in the distance will be *gradually* duller. A neutral will be used for the object or objects located furthest back in space.

IV. VISUALS:

Masaccio, *The Tribute Money* (Figure 11.3)
Botticelli, *The Adoration of the Magi* (Figure 11.14)
Raphael, *The Alba Madonna* (Figure 11.21)

V. MATERIALS AND TOOLS NEEDED FOR THIS LESSON:

Pencils
White drawing paper (23 × 30.5 cm [9 × 12″])
Tempera paint (two complementary colors)
Brushes
Paint cloths
Mixing trays
Water containers

VI. PRESENTATION OF THE LESSON:

A. A discussion of several Renaissance paintings will include a consideration of aerial, or atmospheric, perspective. Students will note how objects furthest back in these paintings are painted in lighter, duller hues.

B. Students are asked to compile an extensive list on the chalkboard of objects that might be included in a landscape painting. After this is done, each student selects at least eight items from this list and arranges these as two-dimensional, overlapping shapes in a landscape composition.

*It is suggested that half the class complete this lesson focusing on gradation in color intensity to suggest space, while the other half of the class completes the preceding lesson (Lesson 11–1), which focuses on value gradation to suggest space.

C. The landscape compositions are then painted with a range of color intensities secured by mixing two complementary colors. Highest intensities will be applied to objects in the foreground. Objects further back in the compositions will be painted in intensities that become gradually duller and duller. The object located furthest back in the composition should be painted with a neutral obtained by mixing equal amounts of the two complementary colors.

VII. EVALUATION OF THE LESSON:

A. RESPONSE:

Having considered the *visual qualities* stressed by *formalism*, did students acknowledge that *Renaissance* artists such as *Masaccio, Botticelli,* and *Raphael* were concerned with creating an illusion of depth in their paintings as a way of making them look more lifelike? Could they define "aerial, or atmospheric, perspective"? Were they able to explain how gradation in color intensity can be used to help achieve the appearance of distance in a painting?

## LESSON 11–2 (Continued)

B. PRODUCTION:

Did students complete a *landscape painting* with *tempera paint* in which all forms are shown as two-dimensional, overlapping *shapes*? Were the shapes in this landscape *painted* in a *variety* of color *intensities* obtained by mixing two complementary colors of their own choosing? Were different intensities of the same hue used to *emphasize* the element of *space*? Did the intensities become gradually duller as students painted objects further and further back into space? Was a neutral used for the object or objects located furthest back in space?

I. TITLE OF THE LESSON: Expanding Detail Drawing

II. DURING THIS LESSON STUDENTS ARE TO ACQUIRE INFORMATION ABOUT THE FOLLOWING:

# LESSON 12–1

| RESPONSE | | | | PRODUCTION | | | | |
|---|---|---|---|---|---|---|---|---|
| Artists or Art Objects | Period or Style | Theories of Art | Aesthetic Qualities | Subject Matter | Elements of Art | Principles of Art | Media | Techniques |
| van Eyck | Northern Renaissance | Imitation-alism | Literal Qualities | Still-Life Object | Line | Emphasis | Pencil | Drawing |
| van der Weyden | | | | | Shape | | | |

III. OBJECTIVES:
  A. RESPONSE:
  Examining paintings by Jan van Eyck and Rogier van der Weyden, students learn that *northern Renaissance* artists continued to exhibit a great concern for details and precision in their paintings. Using *imitationalism* as a guide, students are able to make a thorough inventory of the *literal qualities* evident in the paintings under study.

  B. PRODUCTION:
  Students complete *pencil drawings* in which they begin with a detail found on an interesting and intricate *object* of their own choosing. From this starting point, the drawings expand in all directions as students *draw* the objects in a detailed, precise manner. The *lines* and *shapes* used in these drawings will be complex to *emphasize* the intricate nature of the objects being drawn.*

IV. VISUALS:
  Jan van Eyck, *Giovanni Arnolfini and His Bride* (Figure 12.1), *Adoration of the Lamb* (Figure 12.2)
  Rogier van der Weyden, *Descent from the Cross* (Figure 12.4), *Portrait of a Lady* (Figure 12.5)

V. MATERIALS AND TOOLS NEEDED FOR THIS LESSON:
  Pencils
  White drawing paper (23 × 30.5 cm [9 × 12″])

VI. PRESENTATION OF THE LESSON:
  A. While examining paintings by Jan van Eyck and Rogier van der Weyden, students learn that northern Renaissance artists persisted in seeking precise and accurate details in their artworks.
  B. Prior to this lesson, students were asked to bring to class an "interesting and intricate" object to draw. Among the items they might consider are these: an old, laced boot; a kerosene lantern; a piece of complex machinery.
  C. Beginning at or near the center of the paper, students are instructed to draw as accurately as possible some part of the object. Precision and accuracy are stressed as students add details to their drawing, allowing it to "grow" until it reaches all four edges of the paper. Students are reminded that the lines and shapes used in their drawing should be complex, reflecting and emphasizing the intricate nature of the object being drawn. (If desired, students could also be urged to attend to variety and gradation of value as a further means of enhancing the accuracy of their drawing.)

---

*This lesson may also be used to direct students' attention to *contrast* and *gradation* of *value* as a way of enhancing the accuracy of their drawings.

VII. EVALUATION OF THE LESSON:
   A. RESPONSE:
      Did students recognize the continued concern for detail and precision that marked the artworks of *northern Renaissance* artists such as Jan van Eyck and Rogier van der Weyden? Using *imitationalism* as a guide, were students able to make a thorough inventory of the *literal qualities* evident in the paintings under study?
   B. PRODUCTION:
      Did students complete *pencil drawings* in which they began with a detail found on an interesting and intricate *object* of their own choosing? Were all the objects included in the composition *drawn* in a detailed, precise manner? Were the *lines* and *shapes* used in these drawings complex, to *emphasize* the intricate nature of the objects being drawn?

# LESSON 12–1 (Continued)

I. TITLE OF THE LESSON: Designing a Visual Symbol

II. DURING THIS LESSON STUDENTS ARE TO ACQUIRE INFORMATION ABOUT THE FOLLOWING:

# LESSON 12–2

| RESPONSE | | | | PRODUCTION | | | | |
|---|---|---|---|---|---|---|---|---|
| Artists or Art Objects | Period or Style | Theories of Art | Aesthetic Qualities | Subject Matter | Elements of Art | Principles of Art | Media | Techniques |
| van Eyck<br><br>van der Goes | Northern Renaissance | | | Symbols | Shape<br><br>Value (Non-Color) | Emphasis | India Ink | Design |

III. OBJECTIVES:

  A. RESPONSE:

Students recognize that *northern Renaissance* painters including *Jan van Eyck* and *Hugo van der Goes* placed great importance on symbolism. They can point to examples of symbolism in the works of these artists.

  B. PRODUCTION:

Students *design* and execute in *India ink symbols* for a fictitious organization. These symbols are characterized by the use of simplified *shapes* and bold contrasts of *value* to *emphasize* and draw attention to the design.

IV. VISUALS:

Jan van Eyck, *Giovanni Arnolfini and His Bride* (Figure 12.1), *Adoration of the Lamb* (Figure 12.2)

Hugo van der Goes, *The Adoration of the Shepherds* (Figure 12.6)

V. MATERIALS AND TOOLS NEEDED FOR THIS LESSON:

Pencils
Newsprint
White drawing paper (23 × 30.5 cm [9 × 12″])
India ink
Pens and penholders
Brushes

VI. PRESENTATION OF THE LESSON:

  A. During a discussion of the works of Jan van Eyck and Hugo van der Goes, attention is directed to their use of symbols. Many of the objects found in their paintings were meant to have special meanings beyond those usually associated with the objects.

  B. Students are instructed to design a visual symbol for a fictitious organization. They might, for example, decide to design the symbol for a group calling itself "The Agency to Eliminate Unemployment," or another known as "The Society to Save America's Trees." (The class could decide upon the names of several such organizations during a discussion session devoted to this task.)

  C. Each student compiles a list of words or image statements associated with the name of the organization. In the case of "The Agency to Eliminate Unemployment," they would first identify words or statements that mean the same thing as "eliminate." When that list is complete, they would go on to do the same with the word "unemployment."

  D. The five most descriptive and original words or image statements would then be selected from each list and arranged in a matrix. The words associated with "eliminate" might be placed along the horizontal portion of this matrix, while the words or image statements associated with "unemployment" could be arranged along the vertical. As indicated in the example on page 75, this provides twenty-five different combinations which can be used as starting points by students.

E. After considering their word combinations carefully, each student chooses three that have the most potential and sketches a series of visual symbols for each.

F. The best of the visual-symbol sketches is developed further. Students are advised to eliminate unnecessary details and make their symbols as simple and easy-to-read as possible without destroying their meanings.

G. When they are satisfied with their symbols, students are asked to complete final versions in India ink. Bold contrasts of value are used as a way of drawing attention to these symbols.

VII. EVALUATION OF THE LESSON:

A. RESPONSE:
Did students recognize the importance attached to symbolism by such *northern Renaissance* painters as *Jan van Eyck* and *Hugo van der Goes*? Could they point out examples of symbolism in the work of those artists?

B. PRODUCTION:
Did students design and execute in *India ink symbols* for a fictitious organization? Were these symbols characterized by the use of simplified *shapes* and bold contrasts of *value* to *emphasize* and draw attention to the design?

| ELIMINATE | UNEMPLOYMENT | | | | |
|---|---|---|---|---|---|
| | Idle hands | | | | |
| Crossed out | | | | | |
| | | | | | |
| | | | | | |
| | | | | | |
| | | | | | |

When all the words or image statements have been filled in on a matrix like this, students have twenty-five combinations which can be used as starting points in the creation of visual symbols for "The Agency to Eliminate Unemployment."

I. TITLE OF THE LESSON: Bizarre Creatures from Expanded Paper Shapes

II. DURING THIS LESSON STUDENTS ARE TO ACQUIRE INFORMATION ABOUT THE FOLLOWING:

# LESSON 13–1

| RESPONSE | | | | PRODUCTION | | | | |
|---|---|---|---|---|---|---|---|---|
| Artists or Art Objects | Period or Style | Theories of Art | Aesthetic Qualities | Subject Matter | Elements of Art | Principles of Art | Media | Techniques |
| Dürer Bosch Bruegel | | Emotional-ism | Expressive Qualities | Bizarre Creatures | Shape | Harmony Variety | Paper | Cutting |

III. OBJECTIVES:

A. RESPONSE:

Students observe the unusual creatures often included in the works of *Dürer* and *Bosch*. They also identify the humorous quality that prevails in the highly imaginative paintings of Bosch and *Bruegel*. Referring to the *expressive qualities* stressed by *emotionalism*, they can interpret the ideas, moods, and feelings communicated by the works of all three artists.

B. PRODUCTION:

Students complete expanded-*shape* designs derived from a single, free-form, solid shape *cut* from white *construction paper*. This shape is divided into fifteen smaller units and arranged in such a way that a much larger *harmonious* shape is realized. Details cut from colored construction paper are added to create a *bizarre creature* suggested by the expanded shape. These details should be intricate and *varied* to add interest to the composition.

IV. VISUALS:

Dürer, *Knight, Death, and the Devil* (Figure 13.10)
Bosch, *Death and the Miser* (Figure 13.11)
Bruegel, *The Parable of the Blind* (Figure 13.12)

Students should also be asked to examine additional works by Bosch and Bruegel available in other books.

V. MATERIALS AND TOOLS NEEDED FOR THIS LESSON:

White construction paper (15 × 23 cm [6 × 9″])
Colored construction paper for background (30.5 × 46 cm [12 × 18″])
Scissors
Glue (see Safety Note in text, page 242)

VI. PRESENTATION OF THE LESSON:

A. Students examine and discuss the works of Dürer, Bosch, and Bruegel, noting in particular the highly imaginative creatures and the often humorous incidents found in these works. They are told that they will test their own powers of imagination to create a bizarre, whimsical creature of their own from an expanded-shape design.

B. Students cut a simple, free-form, solid shape from a section of 15 × 23-cm [6 × 9-inch] white construction paper.

C. The free-form shape is cut into three parts, each of which is characterized by curvilinear contours.

D. Each of the three shapes is divided into five curvilinear shapes, resulting in a total of fifteen shapes.

E. All fifteen shapes are now glued to a large (30.5 × 46-cm [12 × 18-inch]) sheet of colored construction paper. Each of these shapes *must* touch the ones it was cut from at some point, but is also expanded.

F. When all fifteen shapes are glued in place, students are asked to examine their designs from every direction. They are told to use their imagination to identify the various bizarre creatures that might be suggested.

G. When such a creature is discovered, details such as eyes, ears, nose, mouth, teeth, legs, tail, etc. cut from colored construction paper are added. (Students should be encouraged to be as original as possible in designing these details.)

H. A colorful and descriptive label or name for each creature is indicated on each completed design. When these works are exhibited, students may also be asked to describe the unusual traits or habits that distinguish their imaginary creatures from real creatures.

VII. EVALUATION OF THE LESSON:

A. RESPONSE:

Did students point out the unusual creatures found in the works of *Dürer* and *Bosch*? Were they able to recognize the humorous quality in the paintings by Bosch and *Bruegel*? Did they refer to the *expressive qualities* stressed by *emotionalism* to interpret the ideas, moods, and feelings communicated by the works of all three artists?

B. PRODUCTION:

Did students complete expanded-*shape* designs derived from a single, free-form, solid shape *cut* from white *paper*? Was this shape divided into fifteen smaller units which were arranged to create a larger *harmonious* shape? Did they use details cut from colored construction paper to suggest a *bizarre creature*? Were these details intricate and *varied* to add interest to the composition?

I. TITLE OF THE LESSON: Modeling Expressive Figures in Clay

II. DURING THIS LESSON STUDENTS ARE TO ACQUIRE INFORMATION ABOUT THE FOLLOWING:

# LESSON 13–2

| RESPONSE | | | | PRODUCTION | | | | |
|---|---|---|---|---|---|---|---|---|
| Artists or Art Objects | Period or Style | Theories of Art | Aesthetic Qualities | Subject Matter | Elements of Art | Principles of Art | Media | Techniques |
| Parmigia-nino Tintoretto El Greco | Mannerism | Emotional-ism | Expressive Qualities | Figures | Form Texture (Actual) | Movement Harmony Variety Proportion | Clay | Modeling |

III. OBJECTIVES:

A. RESPONSE:

When examining *Mannerist* paintings by *Parmigianino*, *Tintoretto*, and *El Greco*, students observe that these artists used exaggeration, distortion, and movement to appeal to the emotions of viewers. Employing *emotionalism* as their guide to the *expressive qualities*, students are able to interpret the moods and feelings communicated by the works of these artists.

B. PRODUCTION:

Students *model* in *clay* seated or reclining *figures* which communicate various emotions or feelings through the use of *movement* and exaggerated, distorted *proportions*. These figures are characterized by *harmonious forms* and a *variety* of *textural* contrasts.

IV. VISUALS:

Parmigianino, *The Madonna with the Long Neck* (Figure 13.4)

Tintoretto, *Presentation of the Virgin* (Figure 13.5)

El Greco, *The Martyrdom of St. Maurice and the Theban Legion* (Figure 13.7), *The Burial of Count Orgaz* (Figure 13.8)

References may also be made to the following works:
*Dying Gaul* (Figure 6.17)
*Seated Boxer* (Figure 6.19)

V. MATERIALS AND TOOLS NEEDED FOR THIS LESSON:

Pencils
Newsprint
Water-base clay
Clay-modeling tools
Slip
Skewers (30.5 cm [12″], used for making kabobs and available in most department and grocery stores)
Pieces of cloth, burlap, or canvas

VI. PRESENTATION OF THE LESSON:

A. During a discussion of Mannerist paintings by Parmigianino, Tintoretto, and El Greco, students observe that these artists used exaggeration, distortion, and movement in an effort to appeal to the emotions of viewers.

B. Students are asked to complete several quick sketches of seated or reclining figures which communicate a particular emotion or feeling. The choice of emotion or feeling is left up to each student, but all students are instructed to use exaggeration, distortion, and movement to amplify the emotion or feeling selected.

C. Students interpret their most effective sketch in clay. Again, they are reminded that exaggeration, distortion, and movement are the major concerns, taking precedence over representational accuracy.

D. A clay block is first modeled to the general size and shape of the torso. Legs and arms formed into general shapes are carefully molded onto this torso. Details are avoided as students attempt to suggest general forms and proportions. At this early stage, a wooden paddle may be used to shape and tie the pieces of the figure together.

E. A small piece of clay is rolled into the shape of the head. This is placed on the body and a coil of clay used to join the two parts together. This coil forms the neck of the figure. A skewer may be used to hold the head in place and help support the figure as work continues. This skewer is kept in place until the figure is ready to be hollowed out.

F. Once the head is in place, the student may turn or tilt it in any direction desired. The arms and legs are also positioned and hands and feet are added. However, students are advised to keep their figures simple and not become overly concerned with unnecessary details. Fingers, toes, facial features, and clothing, for example, should be suggested in a general way only.

G. A modeling tool is used to complete the figure. At this time, attention should be directed to creating variety in the textural surfaces. Various marking and modeling tools can be used, and some students may wish to use an old toothbrush to obtain textural effects.

H. When the piece is almost leather-hard, the skewer is removed. The piece is then carefully hollowed out from the bottom. As much clay as possible should be removed during this hollowing out process.

I. The figure is allowed to dry and is kiln fired.

J. Finished pieces may be rubbed with linseed oil and waxed, or shoe polish (paste or liquid) may be applied and rubbed to a shine with a soft cloth. (Other finishing techniques are suggested in Lesson 10-3.)

# LESSON 13–2 (Continued)

VII. EVALUATION OF THE LESSON:
   A. RESPONSE:
      When examining *Mannerist* paintings by *Parmigianino*, *Tintoretto*, and *El Greco*, did students observe the use of exaggeration, distortion, and movement? Using *emotionalism* as a guide to the *expressive qualities*, were students able to interpret the moods and feelings communicated by the works of these artists?

   B. PRODUCTION:
      Did the seated or reclining *figures* students *modeled* in *clay* communicate emotions or feelings through the use of *movement* and exaggerated, distorted *proportions*? Were these figures characterized by *harmonious forms* and a *variety* of *textural* contrasts?

I. TITLE OF THE LESSON: Drawing a Shape Moving in Space

II. DURING THIS LESSON STUDENTS ARE TO ACQUIRE INFORMATION ABOUT THE FOLLOWING:

# LESSON 14–1

| RESPONSE | | | | PRODUCTION | | | | |
|---|---|---|---|---|---|---|---|---|
| Artists or Art Objects | Period or Style | Theories of Art | Aesthetic Qualities | Subject Matter | Elements of Art | Principles of Art | Media | Techniques |
| Bernini<br><br>Rubens | Baroque | Formalism | Visual Qualities | Falling, Bouncing Geometric Object | Shape<br><br>Space | Movement | Pencil | Drawing |

III. OBJECTIVES:

A. RESPONSE:
Students learn that *Baroque* forms and figures do more than occupy space. Rather, they seem to move about freely in that space. During their discussions of Baroque art, students focus on the *visual qualities* favored by *formalism* to identify the various ways Baroque artists such as *Bernini* and *Rubens* created the illusion of movement or rhythm in space.

B. PRODUCTION:
Students complete a *pencil drawing* which records in repeated, overlapping *shapes* the rhythm or *movement* of a *falling, bouncing geometric object* as it turns and twists through *space*.

IV. VISUALS:
Bernini, *The Ecstasy of St. Theresa* (Figure 14.4)
Rubens, *The Elevation of the Cross* (Figure 14.8)

V. MATERIALS AND TOOLS NEEDED FOR THIS LESSON:
Pencils
White drawing paper (23 × 30.5 cm [9 × 12″])
Rulers (optional)

VI. PRESENTATION OF THE LESSON:

A. While examining examples of artworks by Baroque artists, students observe how the forms and figures appear to twist, turn, and spiral in space. As a result, everything in the paintings seems to be in motion.

B. Each student is asked to draw a simple geometric shape at or near the top left corner of a sheet of white drawing paper. The same shape is drawn again at the lower right corner of the paper.

C. Students are told to imagine that the geometric shape they have drawn is made of rubber. Their picture shows the first and last positions of the shape after it has been dropped and moves through space.

D. They are to make a series of drawings showing the shape as it twists, turns, and bounces through space from its starting point at the upper left corner until it comes to rest at the lower right corner of the paper. Thus, the shape is repeated over and over again. Drawings of the shape will overlap slightly and be placed to suggest a continuous movement through space. At least one bounce should be indicated.

VII. EVALUATION OF THE LESSON:
  A. RESPONSE:
     Did students recognize that the forms and figures in *Baroque* artworks seem to move about freely in space? Concentrating on the *visual qualities* favored by *formalism*, were they able to identify the various ways Baroque artists such as *Bernini* and *Rubens* created the illusion of movement or rhythm in space?
  B. PRODUCTION:
     Did student *pencil drawings* show in repeated, overlapping *shapes* the rhythm or *movement* of a *falling, bouncing geometric object* turning and twisting through *space*?

# LESSON 14–1 (Continued)

I. TITLE OF THE LESSON: Ink Drawings Emphasizing Value Contrasts for Dramatic Effect

II. DURING THIS LESSON STUDENTS ARE TO ACQUIRE INFORMATION ABOUT THE FOLLOWING:

# LESSON 14-2

| RESPONSE | | | | PRODUCTION | | | | |
|---|---|---|---|---|---|---|---|---|
| Artists or Art Objects | Period or Style | Theories of Art | Aesthetic Qualities | Subject Matter | Elements of Art | Principles of Art | Media | Techniques |
| Caravaggio Gentileschi Rembrandt Ribera Velázquez | Baroque | | | Figure | Value (Non-Color) Shape | Emphasis | Pencil India Ink | Drawing Painting |

III. OBJECTIVES:

A. RESPONSE:

Examining *Baroque* paintings by *Caravaggio*, *Gentileschi*, *Rembrandt*, *Ribera*, and *Velázquez*, students recognize how these artists made use of contrasting light and dark values. They can explain how the use of light and dark values heightens the dramatic impact of these paintings. They also note how value contrasts are used to direct the viewer's attention to the most important parts of each work.

B. PRODUCTION:

Students first complete a *pencil drawing* of a model in an action pose. When the model is spotlighted, shadowed areas are revealed, and students *paint* in these areas on their drawing with *India ink* and brush. Bold contrasts of light and dark *values* combined with a use of simplified *shapes* result in an ink *figure drawing* more notable for its dramatic *emphasis* than for its representational accuracy.

IV. VISUALS:

Caravaggio, *The Conversion of St. Paul* (Figure 14.6)

Gentileschi, *Judith and Maidservant with the Head of Holofernes* (Figure 14.7)

Rembrandt, *The Company of Captain Frans Banning Cocq* (or *The Night Watch*) (Figure 14.12)

Ribera, *The Blind Old Beggar* (Figure 14.17)

Velázquez, *Las Meninas* (or *The Maids of Honor*) (Figure 14.20)

V. MATERIALS AND TOOLS NEEDED FOR THIS LESSON:

Pencils

White drawing paper (46 × 61 cm [18 × 24"])

Spotlight

India ink

Brushes (1.3 to 2.54-cm [½ to 1-inch] wide with square tips, as well as smaller brushes with pointed tips)

VI. PRESENTATION OF THE LESSON:

A. Students view and discuss several paintings by Baroque artists, noting how each used light to achieve dramatic effects. They speculate upon the source and the quality of the light in the paintings under study. They also observe how light is used to illustrate the most important parts of each work.

B. A student model on a raised platform or table assumes an active pose (throwing, chopping, pushing, catching, etc.). Students complete a large pencil drawing of this model, concentrating on contours and the more important details. Fine details, textures, and values are not included in these drawings.

C. The room is darkened and students experiment directing a spotlight on the model, who returns to the same action pose as before.

D. A position for the spotlight is agreed upon, and students are asked to paint in the dark value areas on their drawings with India ink. The brushes used for this purpose are approximately 1.3 to 2.54 cm [½ to 1"] in width and have square tips. Students are shown that by using a flat brush the contours are crisp, and unwanted details are eliminated. The sizes of the value areas can be controlled by turning the brush from its thin edge to its widest edge with little change of pressure.

E. Dark values should be painted quickly and spontaneously.

F. Smaller, pointed brushes may be used to emphasize the more important lines of the figure. By varying the pressure on these brushes, contrasting thick and thin lines can be realized.

VII. EVALUATION OF THE LESSON:

A. RESPONSE:

Did students recognize how *Baroque* artists such as *Caravaggio*, *Gentileschi*, *Rembrandt*, *Ribera*, and *Velázquez* made use of contrasting light and dark values in their works? Could they explain how the use of light and dark values heightens the dramatic impact of these paintings? Did they note how value contrasts are used to direct the viewer's attention to the most important parts of each work?

B. PRODUCTION:

Did students complete a *pencil drawing* of a model in an action pose? When shadowed areas were revealed on the spotlighted model, did students *paint* in these areas on their drawing with *India ink* and brush? Were bold contrasts of light and dark *values* combined with a use of simplified *shapes*? And did this result in an ink *figure drawing* more notable for its dramatic *emphasis* than for its representational accuracy?

I. TITLE OF THE LESSON: Still-Life Drawing in Pastels

II. DURING THIS LESSON STUDENTS ARE TO ACQUIRE INFORMATION ABOUT THE FOLLOWING:

# LESSON 15-1

| RESPONSE | | | | PRODUCTION | | | | |
|---|---|---|---|---|---|---|---|---|
| Artists or Art Objects | Period or Style | Theories of Art | Aesthetic Qualities | Subject Matter | Elements of Art | Principles of Art | Media | Techniques |
| Watteau | Rococo | Imitation-alism | Literal Qual-ities | Still Life | Value (Non-Color) | Gradation | Pastels | Drawing |
| Fragonard | | Formalism | Visual Qual-ities | | Form | Emphasis | | |
| Chardin | | | | | Texture (Simulated) | Variety | | |

III. OBJECTIVES:

A. RESPONSE:

Students compare and contrast paintings in the *Rococo* style created by *Watteau* and *Fragonard* with works produced at about the same time by *Chardin*. Employing *imitationalism* as a guide to a study of the *literal qualities*, students recognize that Chardin did not paint the same subject matter as Watteau and Fragonard. Referring to the *visual qualities* favored by *formalism*, they can also identify differences in the artistic style of Chardin when his works are compared to those by Watteau and Fragonard.

B. PRODUCTION:

Students use *pastels* to *draw* a *still-life* composition in which they do the following:

1. Use *gradations* of *value* to *emphasize* the roundness of *forms*.
2. Replicate the *variety* of *textures* observed in the still life.

IV. VISUALS:

Watteau, *Embarkation for Cythera* (Figure 15.2)
Fragonard, *The Swing* (Figure 15.3)
Chardin, *Still Life with Rib of Beef* (Figure 15.4), *The Attentive Nurse* (Figure 15.5)

V. MATERIALS AND TOOLS NEEDED FOR THIS LESSON:

Scissors
Poster board, cardboard, or paper (approximately 15 × 15 cm [6 × 6"])
Neutral-tone drawing paper or construction paper (46 × 61 cm [18 × 24"])*
White chalk
Pastels (colored chalk)
Rulers

VI. PRESENTATION OF THE LESSON:

A. Students examine and discuss works by Watteau, Fragonard, and Chardin. They observe that Chardin preferred to paint humble, common objects such as earthenware containers, copper kettles, and vegetables rather than the elegant court scenes favored by Watteau and Fragonard.

B. Concentrating on Chardin's still-life painting, students note how the artist was able to suggest subtle changes of color, light, and texture.

C. The class is divided into several small groups and instructed to set up several still-life arrangements. To do this, they make use of a variety of common, everyday items brought to class for this purpose.

D. Each student then fashions a simple "viewfinder" by cutting a piece of poster board, cardboard, or paper into two "L" shapes, as shown in Figure 11.

---

*Pastel or chalk drawings are best done on paper with a lightly coarse, abrasive surface. This surface effectively accepts and holds the chalk particles. (See Safety Note in text, page 281.)

E. By manipulating the viewfinder, students are able to alter the views of their still-life arrangements. Some may be pleased with a close-up view of a small portion of the still life. Others may prefer a view that includes all or most of the objects in their still life.

F. Working on large sheets of neutral-tone drawing paper (or construction paper), students lightly draw with white chalk the view they find most pleasing when looking through their viewfinders. They are urged to study carefully the objects they are drawing and to reproduce them as accurately as possible.

G. Pastels are used in the following manner to complete the still-life compositions:
   1. "Base" colors that closely match the colors of the still-life objects are applied first.
   2. Changes of value are achieved by lightening and darkening various parts of the objects. Students are instructed to use value gradation where needed to emphasize the roundness of certain objects.
   3. Students should also seek to reproduce as accurately as possible the various contrasting textural surfaces observed in their still-life objects.
   4. Details and the darkest shading are done last.

H. The completed pastel still-lifes are displayed and discussed in terms of the differing compositions—close-up views can be compared with other views showing the still life from different distances. Also discussed are the uses of light and dark values to suggest roundness of certain three-dimensional forms, and the various textural effects achieved.

# LESSON 15–1 (Continued)

VII. EVALUATION OF THE LESSON:
   A. RESPONSE:
   Did students use *imitationalism* as a guide to a study of the *literal qualities* in works by *Watteau, Fragonard,* and *Chardin*? Were they able to point out the differences in the subject matter preferred by these artists? Referring to the *visual qualities* favored by *formalism,* were students able to identify differences in artistic style when comparing Chardin's work with works completed in the *Rococo* style by Watteau and Fragonard?

   B. PRODUCTION:
   Did students use *pastels* to *draw* a *still-life* composition in which they did the following:
   1. Used *gradations* of *value* to *emphasize* the roundness of *forms*?
   2. Replicated the *variety* of *textures* observed in the still life?

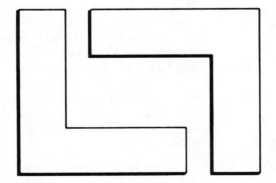 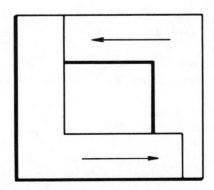

**Figure 11. Viewfinders are made of two "L" shapes joined together and manipulated to alter the views of the subject matter.**

I. TITLE OF THE LESSON: Expressing an Emotion or Mood in an Ink Drawing

II. DURING THIS LESSON STUDENTS ARE TO ACQUIRE INFORMATION ABOUT THE FOLLOWING:

# LESSON 15-2

| RESPONSE | | | | PRODUCTION | | | | |
|---|---|---|---|---|---|---|---|---|
| Artists or Art Objects | Period or Style | Theories of Art | Aesthetic Qualities | Subject Matter | Elements of Art | Principles of Art | Media | Techniques |
| Goya | | Emotionalism | Expressive Qualities | Contemporary Event | Value (Non-Color) | Variety Emphasis | India Ink | Drawing |

III. OBJECTIVES:
  A. RESPONSE:
  Mindful of the *expressive qualities* emphasized by *emotionalism*, students are able to point to and interpret the actions, expressions, and gestures of the figures found in *Goya's* painting, *The Third of May, 1808.*

  B. PRODUCTION:
  Students complete *ink drawings* in which *contemporary events* of their own choosing are illustrated in a dramatic manner. Rather than present objective renditions of these events, students seek to communicate their own personal feelings about them. *Varied,* contrasting *values* of ink washes are applied to these drawings to further *emphasize* the drama depicted.

IV. VISUALS:
  Goya, *The Third of May, 1808* (Figure 15.11)

V. MATERIALS AND TOOLS NEEDED FOR THIS LESSON:
  Newspaper or magazine articles dealing with unusual or dramatic contemporary events
  Pencils
  Newsprint
  India ink
  Pens and penholders
  Brushes
  Mixing trays
  White drawing paper (23 × 30.5 cm [9 × 12″] or larger)
  Water containers
  Paint cloths

VI. PRESENTATION OF THE LESSON:
  A. After a discussion during which students describe, analyze, interpret, and judge Goya's painting of *The Third of May, 1808*, the teacher notes that the dramatic event depicted is based on an actual event.
  B. Each student is asked to find and bring to class a newspaper or magazine article dealing with an unusual or exciting contemporary event.
  C. After students have read their articles out loud, the class selects three that seem most promising as subjects for a dramatic picture to be done in ink and ink wash.
  D. Students complete several pencil sketches in which they try to illustrate the event described in one or more of the articles. In each sketch, students should emphasize the expressive qualities—the works are intended to communicate feelings or moods rather than provide objective illustrations.
  E. The most successful sketches are transferred to white drawing paper. Students are free to select the paper size.
  F. Pencil lines are redrawn with India ink. Some students may opt to use a variety of thick and thin lines.
  G. Ink washes in a range of contrasting values are used to tint various areas or shapes in the pictures. Contrasts of value are used to highlight the drama of the event shown. (Further reference to Goya's painting might be helpful here as the teacher points out how Goya used the glare of a lantern to reveal the actions of the men facing the firing squad.)

H. When the pictures are finished, they are displayed, and class comments are directed to their effectiveness in emphasizing and communicating a particular feeling or mood.

VII. EVALUATION OF THE LESSON:

A. RESPONSE:

Did students concentrate on the *expressive qualities* emphasized by *emotionalism* to point out and interpret the actions, expressions, and gestures of the figures in *Goya*'s painting, *The Third of May, 1808*?

B. PRODUCTION:

Did students complete *ink drawings* in which *contemporary events* are illustrated in a dramatic manner? Were they successful in communicating their personal feelings about these events? Were *varied*, contrasting *values* of ink washes used to *emphasize* the drama depicted?

I. TITLE OF THE LESSON: Watercolor Still Life in the Style of Delacroix

II. DURING THIS LESSON STUDENTS ARE TO ACQUIRE INFORMATION ABOUT THE FOLLOWING:

# LESSON 16–1

| RESPONSE | | | | PRODUCTION | | | | |
|---|---|---|---|---|---|---|---|---|
| Artists or Art Objects | Period or Style | Theories of Art | Aesthetic Qualities | Subject Matter | Elements of Art | Principles of Art | Media | Techniques |
| Ingres | Neoclassic | Formalism | Visual Qualities | Still Life | Hue | Variety | Water-color | Painting |
| Delacroix | Romantic | | | | Line | | | |

III. OBJECTIVES:

A. RESPONSE:

Students examine paintings created by *Ingres* and *Delacroix* and compare and contrast the artistic styles of these two artists. When doing this, they refer to *formalism* and the *visual qualities*. They recognize that Ingres' painting is typical of the *Neoclassic* style and Delacroix's painting is representative of the *Romantic* style. Students are also able to list the major features of both of these art styles and can point to these features in paintings under study.

B. PRODUCTION:

Students *paint still lifes* in *watercolor* in which the shapes of objects are shown as areas of *color (hue)*. These areas of color are created by using a painterly technique in which objects are painted without the aid of preliminary contour lines. Students paint every object in their still lifes by beginning at the center and working outward to the edges. A *variety* of contrasting thick and thin contour *lines* are added only after all painting has been completed.

IV. VISUALS:

Ingres, *Madame Moitessier* (Figure 16.4)
Delacroix, *The Lion Hunt* (Figure 16.6)

V. MATERIALS AND TOOLS NEEDED FOR THIS LESSON:

White drawing paper (or watercolor paper)
Watercolors
Brushes
Water containers
Mixing trays
Paint cloths
India ink
Pens and penholders (brushes may be used instead)

VI. PRESENTATION OF THE LESSON:

A. Students examine paintings by Ingres and Delacroix and compare the differing styles of these two artists. In response to teacher questioning, students recall that Ingres believed that the most important element of art is line and that color was a secondary consideration. Delacroix disagreed and placed greater emphasis on color. Rather than begin his paintings with lines, Delacroix used colors which he worked from the center of his shapes to the edges. Students are told that in the painting experience to follow, they will employ the same approach as Delacroix.

B. A still-life arrangement of five or more objects is set up so all members of the class can view it from their work stations.

C. Working with watercolors, students paint the still life, beginning with the objects closest to them. As they paint each object, they are required to start in the center and work outward to the edges. The entire paper is to be filled in this manner.

D. When the watercolor has dried, contour lines for the various shapes are added with pen and India ink (brushes may be used instead). These contour lines should be as accurate as possible in defining the objects in the still life and should not merely encircle the areas of different colors. Some colors will extend beyond the contour lines, while others may fail to reach the contour lines. This will not have an adverse effect, however. Rather, it represents a feature of the painterly style, which emphasizes the application of color without the aid of preliminary, precise contour lines.

E. Additional ink lines may be added to show various details noted in the still-life objects.

VII. EVALUATION OF THE LESSON:

A. RESPONSE:

Did students compare and contrast the artistic styles of *Ingres* and *Delacroix*? When doing this, did they refer to *formalism* and the *visual qualities*? Could they identify the painting by Ingres as being typical of the *Neoclassic* style? Was Delacroix's painting recognized as an example of the *Romantic* style? Were students able to list the major features of both these art styles? Could they point to these features in the paintings under study?

B. PRODUCTION:

Did students *paint still lifes* in *watercolor* in which the shapes of objects were shown as areas of *color* (*hue*)? Were areas of color created by using a painterly technique in which objects were painted without the aid of preliminary contour lines? Did students paint the objects in their still lifes by beginning at the center and working outward to the edges? Were a *variety* of contrasting thick and thin contour *lines* added after the painting had been completed?

I. TITLE OF THE LESSON: Landscape Painting in the Style of Impressionism

II. DURING THIS LESSON STUDENTS ARE TO ACQUIRE INFORMATION ABOUT THE FOLLOWING:

# LESSON 16–2

| RESPONSE | | | | PRODUCTION | | | | |
|---|---|---|---|---|---|---|---|---|
| **Artists or Art Objects** | **Period or Style** | **Theories of Art** | **Aesthetic Qualities** | **Subject Matter** | **Elements of Art** | **Principles of Art** | **Media** | **Techniques** |
| Monet | Impressionism | | | Landscape | Hue | Variety | Tempera Paint | Painting |
| Renoir | | | | | Texture (Actual) | Emphasis | | |

III. OBJECTIVES:
   A. RESPONSE:
   Students are able to identify correctly works of art done in the *Impressionist style* and can point out the main features of this style in paintings completed by *Monet* and *Renoir*.

   B. PRODUCTION:
   Students complete *landscape paintings* characterized by a *variety* of *hues* applied as dabs and dashes of *tempera paint*. Richly *textured* surfaces are obtained by painting with short brushstrokes. These textured surfaces will contrast with the smooth surface of the posters on which the paintings are mounted. In this way, the textured surface will be *emphasized*.

IV. VISUALS:
   Monet, *Rouen Cathedral* (Figure 16.13), *Haystack at Sunset Near Giverny* (Figure 16.14)
   Renoir, *A Girl with a Watering Can* (Figure 3.3)

V. MATERIALS AND TOOLS NEEDED FOR THIS LESSON:
   Colored photo posters of landscapes (approximately 46 × 30.5 cm [18 × 12″])
   White drawing paper (23 × 30.5 cm [9 × 12″])
   Tempera paints
   Brushes
   Mixing trays
   Water containers
   Paint cloths
   Masking tape

VI. PRESENTATION OF THE LESSON:
   A. Paintings by Monet and Renoir are examined and discussed. Students are asked to list and point to the main features of the Impressionist style found in the works of these two artists. (Reference might be made to the list of features provided in the text on page 303.)

   B. Each student brings to class a large photo poster of a landscape. Posters for this purpose can be purchased in most large department stores as well as novelty, book, and record shops.

   C. Sheets of white drawing paper are attached securely to the posters with pieces of rolled masking tape. Students may attach this paper wherever they desire.

   D. Students "complete" their pictures by painting in the concealed sections of the photo on the white paper. However, they are asked to emulate as closely as possible the Impressionist style as practiced by artists such as Monet and Renoir. When doing this, they should refer often to the list of features completed during the discussion. Particular attention should be directed to the following:
      1. Realizing a variety of hues applied as dabs and dashes of paint.
      2. Replacing the smooth, slick surface of the poster with a contrasting, rich-textured surface.

   E. When completed, the paintings are displayed and students observe and discuss the visual effects. In particular, they note how hues applied in dabs and dashes seem to blend together in the eye of the viewer when seen at a distance.*

---

*An experience in photography has also been included (at the end of Lesson 16–2) as an expansion of the lesson on Impressionism.

## VII. EVALUATION OF THE LESSON:

### A. RESPONSE:
Were students able to identify artworks completed in the *Impressionist style*? Could they point out the main features of this style of painting in works completed by *Monet* and *Renoir*?

### B. PRODUCTION:
Did students complete *landscape paintings* characterized by a *variety* of *hues* applied as dabs and dashes of *tempera paint*? Were short brushstrokes used to create richly *textured* surfaces? Did these textured surfaces contrast with the smooth surface of the posters on which the paintings were mounted? Was the textured surface *emphasized* as a result?

## EXPANSION OF LESSON 16–2: PHOTOGRAPHY

In classes equipped for photography, the teacher may decide to follow up this lesson with another designed to develop student skills with a camera (even a simple camera will do) while assessing the students' knowledge and understanding of the Impressionist style.

Following a reexamination of works by Monet and Renoir, each student is asked to conduct an individual survey outside of class aimed at identifying the "ideal Impressionist scene." At least six black-and-white photographs would be taken of this scene from the same vantage point at different times of the day. These photographs would reflect the student's efforts to record the changing effects of sunlight on subject matter in terms of values only. A careful record would be made of the hour at which each photograph was taken.

# LESSON 16–2 (Continued)

The photographs would be brought to class and exhibited randomly without reference to the time of day they were taken. A discussion might then be initiated by asking students to determine the approximate time of day each photograph was shot. During this discussion, the photographer of each set of prints would be expected to explain why his or her scene might appeal to an Impressionist as the subject for a painting. The photographer would also be expected to reveal the hour at which each photograph was made, provide a detailed explanation of the colors observed in the actual scene, and describe in detail the ways these colors changed as the light conditions varied.

The remainder of the lesson, which could consist of several class sessions, would be devoted to student efforts to paint one (or more) of the photographs in the Impressionist style. Students would be asked to complete a painting that gives the impression of a fleeting moment in time captured not on film, but in a painting, in a manner reminiscent of a Monet or a Renoir.

I. TITLE OF THE LESSON: Designing a Painting Based on van Gogh's *The Potato Eaters*

II. DURING THIS LESSON STUDENTS ARE TO ACQUIRE INFORMATION ABOUT THE FOLLOWING:

# LESSON 17–1

| RESPONSE | | | | PRODUCTION | | | | |
|---|---|---|---|---|---|---|---|---|
| Artists or Art Objects | Period or Style | Theories of Art | Aesthetic Qualities | Subject Matter | Elements of Art | Principles of Art | Media | Techniques |
| van Gogh | | Imitation-alism Formalism Emotional-ism | Literal, Visual, Expressive Qualities | | | | Tempera (or Acrylic) Paint | Painting |

III. OBJECTIVES:

A. RESPONSE:

Examining *van Gogh's* painting of *The Potato Eaters*, students use *imitationalism* to describe its *literal qualities* and *formalism* to analyze its *visual qualities*. They are also able to present and support their interpretations concerning the ideas and feelings communicated by this work. When doing so, they refer to the *expressive qualities* stressed by *emotionalism*.

B. PRODUCTION:

Students complete *paintings* in *tempera* guided by no less than five answers provided previously in a game-playing quiz involving van Gogh's painting of *The Potato Eaters*.

IV. VISUALS:

van Gogh, *The Potato Eaters* (Figure 17.5)

V. MATERIALS AND TOOLS NEEDED FOR THIS LESSON:

Pencils
Newsprint (for preliminary sketches)
White drawing paper or canvas board (no less than 23 × 30.5 cm [9 × 12″])
Tempera (or acrylic) paint
Brushes
Paint cloths
Water containers
Mixing trays

VI. PRESENTATION OF THE LESSON:

A. Students view Vincent van Gogh's painting entitled *The Potato Eaters* and, as a group, respond to the following questions dealing with the literal, visual, and expressive qualities in this work.

*LITERAL QUALITIES*

1. How many people are in this picture?
2. What are these people doing?
3. What kind of clothing are the people wearing?
4. From what you can see, how would you describe this home?
5. How would you describe the economic condition of this family?

*VISUAL QUALITIES*

6. Which color or colors dominate in this picture?
7. Are the values used in this picture dark or light?
8. What textures can you identify in this picture?
9. How would you describe the quality of the line used?
10. What has been done to direct the viewer's eyes to the main parts of the painting?

*EXPRESSIVE QUALITIES*

11. Do you think this home is warm and cozy, or cold and uncomfortable?
12. What word best describes the expressions on the faces of these people?
13. How do you think these people feel at this moment?
14. What might cause them to feel this way?
15. What feelings or moods does this work evoke in you?

B. Using their responses to *at least five* of the questions above as a guide, students design and paint a picture in tempera.

C. When the paintings are completed, they are all exhibited and the class attempts to determine which answers were dealt with in each.

VII. EVALUATION OF THE LESSON:

A. RESPONSE:

Did students use *imitationalism* to describe the *literal qualities* and *formalism* to analyze the *visual qualities* in *van Gogh*'s painting of *The Potato Eaters*? Did the students' interpretations of this work take into account the *expressive qualities* stressed by *emotionalism*?

B. PRODUCTION:

Did students complete *paintings* in *tempera*? Were the students guided by no less than five answers provided previously during a game-playing quiz involving van Gogh's painting of *The Potato Eaters*?

I. TITLE OF THE LESSON: Tempera Batik in the Style of Gauguin

II. DURING THIS LESSON STUDENTS ARE TO ACQUIRE INFORMATION ABOUT THE FOLLOWING:

# LESSON 17–2

| RESPONSE | | | | PRODUCTION | | | | |
|---|---|---|---|---|---|---|---|---|
| **Artists or Art Objects** | **Period or Style** | **Theories of Art** | **Aesthetic Qualities** | **Subject Matter** | **Elements of Art** | **Principles of Art** | **Media** | **Techniques** |
| Gauguin | | Imitation-alism<br><br>Formalism | Literal Qualities<br><br>Visual Qualities | Contemporary Life-style | Shape Intensity Line Space | Variety Harmony | Tempera Paint | Batik |

III. OBJECTIVES:

A. RESPONSE:

Students focus on the *literal qualities* stressed by *imitationalism* to identify and describe the exotic subject matter that characterized many of the paintings by *Gauguin*. Concentrating on the *visual qualities* emphasized by *formalism*, they also observe the ways this artist used the elements of color, shape, and line in his paintings. Students are able to identify the features of Gauguin's decorative painting style including his use of the following:

1. Flat, overlapping shapes.
2. Intense colors.
3. Curving contour lines.

B. PRODUCTION:

Students complete *tempera batiks* in which they present their versions of *life in contemporary society* intended for viewers who are unfamiliar with this contemporary society. They use large, flat *shapes* of *intense color* and overlap these to create the illusion of shallow depth or *space*. *Varied lines* of contrasting thicknesses are used to define the contours of the shapes. The finished pictures reveal that students were more concerned with realizing a flat, decorative, *harmonious* pattern of shapes, colors, and lines than in achieving representational accuracy.

IV. VISUALS:

Gauguin, *Fatata te Miti* (Figure 17.9)
Reference may also be made to *Spirit of the Dead Watching* (Figure 17.8)

V. MATERIALS AND TOOLS NEEDED FOR THIS LESSON:

Pencils
Newsprint
Colored construction paper (23 × 30.5 cm [9 × 12″])
White chalk
Tempera paints
Brushes
Mixing trays
Water containers
Paint cloths
India ink
Trays (or some other flat surface)

VI. PRESENTATION OF THE LESSON:

A. Gauguin's painting is examined and discussed in terms of its literal and visual qualities. Students observe how flat, overlapping shapes of bright color are used to draw the viewer into the work and create the illusion of shallow space.

B. Students consider Gauguin's desire to find and record a way of life unlike the one he knew in Europe. They are asked to complete several sketches in which they present their versions of life in contemporary society. However, their views of contemporary life are to be directed to an audience that has no knowledge at all of this contemporary lifestyle. In fact, this audience will be composed of people living on a remote South Sea island not unlike those visited by Gauguin.

(Thus, while Gauguin sought to portray life as it existed on a remote South Sea paradise for Western viewers, students will do the opposite. They will attempt to show life in the United States today to viewers residing on an isolated South Sea island.)

C. Students reproduce their most successful sketches on sheets of lightly colored construction paper.\* This is done lightly in pencil. The entire sheet of paper is filled and, in some places, the design may even go beyond the edge of the paper. Overlapping shapes are used to suggest shallow space in these pictures.

D. Students go over the main contour lines in their pictures with white chalk. Particular attention is given to the curved contour lines. The quality of the chalk lines is enhanced as students make use of contrasting thick and thin lines.

E. The compositions are painted with a *heavy* application of tempera paint.\*\* Intense hues are employed and dull, dark hues are avoided. During the painting procedure, students are told to paint up to, but not over, the chalk lines. They are also informed that these chalk lines as well as all unpainted areas will be blackened by India ink later.

F. As soon as the tempera paint is dry, each picture is covered completely with a coating of India ink.

G. When the India ink has dried thoroughly, each picture is placed on a tray (or some other flat surface) to prevent it from tearing and the ink is gently washed from the painted surface at the sink. A light stream of water and careful rubbing with the fingers is required. However, students should be cautioned not to remove all the ink from painted surfaces. To do so eliminates much of the batik-like character of this process.

H. If retouching is called for, it can be done while the surface of the picture is still wet. Small amounts of tempera paint can be applied with a sponge or a crushed paper towel.

---

\*Sheets of lightly colored construction paper are used in order that the white chalk lines to be added later will be visible.

---

\*\*A thick coating of tempera paint is required since some will wash off later. Overlapping paint layers is avoided since the top layer will be lost during the final operation. Tempera paint details should never be applied to a previously painted surface.

# LESSON 17–2 (Continued)

VII. EVALUATION OF THE LESSON:
  A. RESPONSE:
    Did students use *imitationalism* as a guide to focus on the *literal qualities in Gauguin*'s painting? Concentrating on the *visual qualities* emphasized by *formalism*, did they observe the ways this artist used the elements of color, shape, and line in his painting? Were they able to identify the features of Gauguin's decorative painting style? Did they make mention of his use of the following:
    1. Flat, overlapping shapes?
    2. Intense colors?
    3. Curving contour lines?

  B. PRODUCTION:
    Did students complete *tempera batiks* in which they presented their versions of *life in contemporary society*? Did they use large, flat *shapes* of *intense color* and overlap these to create the illusion of shallow depth or *space*? Were *varied lines* of contrasting thicknesses used to define the contours of the shapes? Did the finished pictures demonstrate that students were more concerned with realizing a flat, decorative, *harmonious* pattern of shapes, colors, and lines than in achieving representational accuracy?

I. TITLE OF THE LESSON: Drawing in the Cubist Style

II. DURING THIS LESSON STUDENTS ARE TO ACQUIRE INFORMATION ABOUT THE FOLLOWING:

# LESSON 18–1

| RESPONSE | | | | PRODUCTION | | | | |
|---|---|---|---|---|---|---|---|---|
| Artists or Art Objects | Period or Style | Theories of Art | Aesthetic Qualities | Subject Matter | Elements of Art | Principles of Art | Media | Techniques |
| Picasso Braque | Cubism | | | Familiar Object— Abstracted | Line Shape | Variety Harmony | Pencil | Drawing |

III. OBJECTIVES:
   A. RESPONSE:
   Students learn that *Cubism* is a twentieth-century art style in which artists like *Picasso* and *Braque* sought to paint three-dimensional objects as if seen from many different angles at the same time.

   B. PRODUCTION:
   Students will *draw* in *pencil* abstract compositions in the Cubist style. Each composition will consist of sections extracted from preliminary drawings of a *familiar object* seen from different points of view. The finished drawings will consist of a *varied* and *harmonious* arrangement of *lines* and *shapes*.

IV. VISUALS:
   Picasso, *Glass of Absinthe* (Figure 18.10), *Guernica* (Figure 18.11)
   Braque, *Blue Guitar* (Figure 18.13)

V. MATERIALS AND TOOLS NEEDED FOR THIS LESSON:
   Pencils
   Newsprint
   White drawing paper (30.5 × 46 cm [12 × 18″])

VI. PRESENTATION OF THE LESSON:
   A. Works by Picasso and Braque are examined and discussed. Students consider how these Cubist artists sought to paint three-dimensional objects as if seen from several different angles at the same time. Often, as in Picasso's *Glass of Absinthe*, they created works of art which were so abstract that the identity of the objects in them was lost to viewers.

   B. Each student brings to class a familiar object which is to be used as the subject of a Cubist composition. Interesting subjects for this activity include a coffee cup, an unusually shaped bottle or jug, a tennis shoe, or a musical instrument.

   C. With pencil, students complete a series of precise and detailed line drawings of the objects brought to class. Each of these drawings offers a different view of the object. Thus, drawings are done which show the top, bottom, and sides. Students are to refrain from adding values to these line drawings.

   D. All the finished drawings are displayed and discussed. Students are asked to identify those sections of each drawing which seem especially interesting, or which provide the most characteristic features of the object. If desired, heavier lines may be drawn around these portions of the drawings.

   E. Students retrieve their drawings and use them as the basis for their Cubist compositions. These compositions consist of a careful arrangement of the most interesting and characteristic sections extracted from the preliminary drawings. Students are required to include one or more sections selected from every preliminary drawing. In this way, the top, bottom, and sides of the object are included in the final composition.

   F. By joining together and overlapping the various views of their objects, students are able to fashion an intricate and complex abstract composition. These compositions will be composed of a wide array of intricate lines and shapes.

G. In some cases, the complexity of the compositions may obscure the identity of the objects depicted. In other cases, the objects might be ascertained only after careful scrutiny.

VII. EVALUATION OF THE LESSON:

A. RESPONSE:

Did students learn that *Cubism* is a twentieth-century art style? Did they recognize that Cubists like *Picasso* and *Braque* tried to paint three-dimensional objects as if seen from many different angles at the same time?

B. PRODUCTION:

Were students successful in *drawing* with *pencil* abstract compositions in the Cubist style? Did each of their compositions consist of sections extracted from preliminary drawings of a *familiar object* seen from different points of view? Did their finished drawings consist of a *varied* and *harmonious* arrangement of *lines* and *shapes*?

I. TITLE OF THE LESSON: Painting in the Cubist Style

II. DURING THIS LESSON STUDENTS ARE TO ACQUIRE INFORMATION ABOUT THE FOLLOWING:

# LESSON 18–2

| RESPONSE | | | | PRODUCTION | | | | |
|---|---|---|---|---|---|---|---|---|
| **Artists or Art Objects** | **Period or Style** | **Theories of Art** | **Aesthetic Qualities** | **Subject Matter** | **Elements of Art** | **Principles of Art** | **Media** | **Techniques** |
| Picasso | Cubism | Formalism | Visual Qualities | | Value (Non-Color) | Variety Balance (Asymmetrical) Emphasis (Gradation) | Tempera Paint | Painting |

III. OBJECTIVES:

A. RESPONSE:

Students refer to the *visual qualities* favored by *formalism* to learn that, as the *Cubist style* of painting developed, artists like *Picasso* turned to a limited range of browns and grays for coloring in their work.

B. PRODUCTION:

Students *paint* the Cubist compositions developed in the previous lesson (Lesson 18–1). In doing so, they will use a *variety* of light and dark *values* obtained by mixing white and black *tempera paints*. No less than five values will be repeated throughout the composition, and these will be distributed in such a way that an *asymmetrical balance* is realized. *Emphasis* will be realized by employing contrasts of value in certain areas. (Some students may opt to include *gradation* of value as another way of adding interest to their paintings.)

IV. VISUALS:

Picasso, *Glass of Absinthe* (Figure 18.10), *Guernica* (Figure 18.11)

V. MATERIALS AND TOOLS NEEDED FOR THIS LESSON:

Cubist drawings from the previous lesson (Lesson 18–1)
Tempera paints (black and white only)
Brushes
Mixing trays
Water containers
Paint cloths

VI. PRESENTATION OF THE LESSON:

A. Picasso's paintings are examined and attention directed to the lack of color in each. Students observe that the colors associated with the objects depicted in *Glass of Absinthe* are rejected in favor of grays, browns, and other drab tones. In *Guernica*, blacks, whites, and grays are used.

B. Students paint the Cubist drawings completed in the previous lesson, using a range of values obtained by mixing black and white tempera paint.*

1. A minimum of five different values will be repeated throughout the compositions.

2. Contrasts of value will be employed as a means of emphasizing certain parts of their compositions.

3. Students are given the option of using gradation of value in addition to contrast of value to add further interest to their paintings.

---

*Teachers might opt to use a monochromatic color scheme in this studio experience.

4. Concern should be directed at securing asymmetrically balanced compositions.

5. Areas in which white is desired may be left unpainted.

6. Care is to be exercised in painting each shape in the composition so that contours are crisp and smooth.

7. Since an opaque (rather than transparent) effect is sought, students should avoid adding too much water to their tempera paints.

VII. EVALUATION OF THE LESSON:

A. RESPONSE:

Did students refer to the *visual qualities* favored by *formalism* to learn that *Cubist* artists like *Picasso* used a limited range of browns and grays to color their works?

B. PRODUCTION:

Did students *paint* their Cubist compositions with a *variety* of *values* obtained by mixing white and black *tempera paints*? Did they use at least five values, and were these values repeated throughout the composition? Were the paintings *asymmetrically balanced*? Was *emphasis* realized through the use of value contrasts? (Did some students also use *gradation* of value to add interest to their paintings?)

I. TITLE OF THE LESSON: Expressive Paper-Cylinder Faces

II. DURING THIS LESSON STUDENTS ARE TO ACQUIRE INFORMATION ABOUT THE FOLLOWING:

# LESSON 18–3

| RESPONSE | | | | PRODUCTION | | | | |
|---|---|---|---|---|---|---|---|---|
| Artists or Art Objects | Period or Style | Theories of Art | Aesthetic Qualities | Subject Matter | Elements of Art | Principles of Art | Media | Techniques |
| Rouault Kirchner Munch | Expressionism | Emotionalism | Expressive Qualities | Expressive Faces | Form Texture (Actual and Simulated) | Variety Proportion | Colored Construction Paper | Construction |

III. OBJECTIVES:

A. RESPONSE:
   Students learn that the *Expressionists* were artists who wished to share particular emotions or moods with viewers through their art. Concentrating on the *expressive qualities* stressed by *emotionalism*, students are able to identify these emotions or moods in paintings by *Rouault, Kirchner,* and *Munch.*

B. PRODUCTION:
   Students *construct* three-dimensional *faces*, beginning with a cylinder formed with *colored construction paper*. These faces are to exhibit a particular character demonstrating a specific emotion. Exaggerated *proportions* should be used to emphasize that emotion. Concern should also center on the creation of a *variety* of contrasting actual and simulated *textures* applied to the face *form.*

IV. VISUALS:
   Rouault, *The Old King* (Figure 18.3)
   Kirchner, *Street, Berlin* (Figure 18.4)
   Munch, *The Sick Child* (Figure 18.6)
   References may also be made to the following works:
   Kollwitz, *Death and the Mother* (Figure 18.5)
   Munch, *The Scream* (Figure 18.7)

V. MATERIALS AND TOOLS NEEDED FOR THIS LESSON:
   Colored construction paper (30.5 × 46 cm [12 × 18″])
   Stapler
   Glue
   Scrap pieces of colored construction paper
   Scrap pieces of cloth, yarn, cotton, etc.

VI. PRESENTATION OF THE LESSON:

A. Students examine several works of art created by artists associated with the Expressionist movement. They observe in particular how these artists portrayed people expressing various moods or feelings.

B. At the chalkboard, the teacher compiles a list of colorful occupations under the heading "nouns." These occupations are solicited from members of the class. Next, lists of adjectives, verbs, and adverbs are completed in the same manner. The more items in each list the better, and students are urged to be as inventive as possible. For example, see chart on facing page.

C. Each student then selects a sheet of colored construction paper, rolls it into a cylinder, and staples it. (The paper may be rolled to form a tall, narrow cylinder or a short, wide cylinder.)

D. Using scrap pieces of colored construction paper, cloth, yarn, cotton, and other items, students create unique expressive faces on the cylinder. They identify their own characters by making a single selection from each of the four lists on the chalkboard. Thus, one student might select "Happy Professor Laughing Loudly," while another might choose "Angry Pirate Shouting Frantically." However, students are asked to make their selections silently and not to reveal them to other members of the class.

E. Completed three-dimensional faces should do the following:

1. Portray a character in a specific occupation or role exhibiting in an exaggerated way a particular emotion and action.
2. Reveal a concern for a variety of actual and simulated textural effects.
3. Alter or conceal the basic cylinder form from which it was constructed.

F. The completed cylinder faces are exhibited, and members of the class attempt to identify the emotions and actions demonstrated by each.

VII. EVALUATION OF THE LESSON:

A. RESPONSE:

Did students learn that the *Expressionists* were artists who wished to share particular emotions or moods with viewers through their art? By concentrating on the *expressive qualities* stressed by *emotionalism*, were students able to identify the emotions or moods of characters found in paintings by *Rouault*, *Kirchner*, and *Munch*?

B. PRODUCTION:

Were students successful in *constructing* three-dimensional *faces* from cylinders formed with *colored construction paper*? Did these faces exhibit a particular character demonstrating a specific emotion? Were exaggerated *proportions* used to emphasize that emotion? Were a *variety* of actual and simulated *textures* applied to the face *form*?

| Nouns (Occupations) | Adjectives | Verbs* | Adverbs |
|---|---|---|---|
| Clown | Sad | Frown(ing) | Loudly |
| Pirate | Happy | Laugh(ing) | Violently |
| Cowboy | Angry | Sleep(ing) | Merrily |
| Professor | Lazy | Shout(ing) | Vigorously |
| Policeman | Confused | Cry(ing) | Frantically |

*Add "ing" to each for purposes of this lesson.

(Continued on next page)

Paper-cylinder faces (secondary-level student work)

I. TITLE OF THE LESSON: Drawing Expressive Portraits

II. DURING THIS LESSON STUDENTS ARE TO ACQUIRE INFORMATION ABOUT THE FOLLOWING:

# LESSON 19–1

| RESPONSE | | | | PRODUCTION | | | | |
|---|---|---|---|---|---|---|---|---|
| Artists or Art Objects | Period or Style | Theories of Art | Aesthetic Qualities | Subject Matter | Elements of Art | Principles of Art | Media | Techniques |
| de Kooning | Abstract Expressionism | Emotionalism | Expressive Qualities | Expressive Portraits | Line Shape | Proportion Variety | Pencil | Drawing |

III. OBJECTIVES:

A. RESPONSE:

Students recognize that contemporary artists no longer feel compelled to paint only the outside appearances of their subjects. Using *emotionalism* as a guide to the *expressive qualities*, they can interpret the meaning and mood of an *Abstract Expressionist* painting by *de Kooning*.

B. PRODUCTION:

Students use a continuous *line* to *draw expressive portraits*. In these portraits, they are to exaggerate the *proportions* and expressions of the face and thus record and intensify the inner feelings suggested by those features and expressions. A continuous *pencil* line serves to break the portraits into a *variety* of complex *shapes*.

IV. VISUALS:

de Kooning, *Woman VI* (Figure 19.15)

References may also be made to the following works:

Rouault, *The Old King* (Figure 18.3)
Kirchner, *Street, Berlin* (Figure 18.4)
Munch, *The Scream* (Figure 18.7)

Comparisons can be made to the following works:

Vigée-Lebrun, *Madame de la Châtre* (Figure 16.3)
Ingres, *Madame Moitessier* (Figure 16.4)
Goya, *The Marquesa de Pontejos* (Figure 15.10)

V. MATERIALS AND TOOLS NEEDED FOR THIS LESSON:

"Inner feelings" cards
Pencils
White drawing paper (30.5 × 46 cm [12 × 18 ″])

VI. PRESENTATION OF THE LESSON:

A. Students examine and discuss de Kooning's *Woman VI* noting how it represents a departure from traditional portraits of women by such artists as Vigée-Lebrun, Ingres, and Goya. Students observe that the earlier paintings concentrated on external appearances, while de Kooning's portrait sought to reveal the person within—her inner feelings or emotions.

B. On the chalkboard (or with the aid of an overhead projector) the teacher demonstrates a continuous-line drawing technique in which a face and all its features are recorded with a single pencil line. This continuous line serves to break the face up into a variety of complex shapes.

C. A box or bag is passed around the room, and students are asked to blindly select one of the cards within. Each card lists an inner feeling or emotion, such as "happy," "sad," "depressed," "lonely," "jealous," or "angry." Students are told not to reveal the inner feeling indicated on the cards they select.

D. The class is divided into teams of two. Time is allowed for each team to discuss the inner feelings noted on their cards. Then one team member, acting as a model, assumes the facial expression associated with the inner feeling indicated on his or her card. The other team member draws the face in one continuous line, making sure to fill the entire sheet of paper with this drawing.

E. The expressions and facial features are to be *distorted* and *exaggerated* in order to capture the inner feeling being modeled.

F. When the drawing is finished, the students reverse roles and a second drawing is completed. A new expression reflecting the inner feelings indicated on the second card is modeled and drawn.

VII. EVALUATION OF THE LESSON:

A. RESPONSE:
Did students recognize that contemporary artists no longer feel compelled to paint only the outside appearances of their subjects? Did they use *emotionalism* as a guide to the *expressive qualities* and thus interpret the meaning and mood of an *Abstract Expressionist* painting by *de Kooning*?

B. PRODUCTION:
Was a continuous *line* used by students to *draw expressive portraits*? Did they exaggerate the *proportions* and expressions in these portraits in order to record and intensify the inner feelings suggested by those features and portraits? Did the continuous *pencil* line serve to break the portraits into a *variety* of complex *shapes*?

I. TITLE OF THE LESSON: Coloring Expressive Portraits with Oil Pastels

II. DURING THIS LESSON STUDENTS ARE TO ACQUIRE INFORMATION ABOUT THE FOLLOWING:

# LESSON 19–2

| RESPONSE | | | | PRODUCTION | | | | |
|---|---|---|---|---|---|---|---|---|
| Artists or Art Objects | Period or Style | Theories of Art | Aesthetic Qualities | Subject Matter | Elements of Art | Principles of Art | Media | Techniques |
| de Kooning | | Emotionalism | Expressive Qualities | Expressive Portraits | Hue | Emphasis | Oil Pastels | |

III. OBJECTIVES:

A. RESPONSE:

Referring again to the *expressive qualities* stressed by *emotionalism* when examining *de Kooning*'s painting of *Woman VI*, students recognize that colors are often used in pictures to emphasize or heighten a mood or feeling.

B. PRODUCTION:

Students use *oil pastels* to color the *expressive portraits* completed in the previous lesson (Lesson 19-1). When doing so, they make certain that the *hues* selected will complement and *emphasize* the inner feelings portrayed.

IV. VISUALS:

de Kooning, *Woman VI* (Figure 19.15)

References may also be made to the following works:

Picasso, *The Blind Man's Meal* (Figure 18.12)
van Gogh, *The Potato Eaters* (Figure 17.5)

V. MATERIALS AND TOOLS NEEDED FOR THIS LESSON:

Expressive portraits from the previous lesson (Lesson 19–1)
Oil pastels

VI. PRESENTATION OF THE LESSON:

A. Students again examine and discuss de Kooning's painting of *Woman VI*, concentrating on its expressive use of color. Works by Picasso and van Gogh may also be viewed, and students observe how those artists also used color to accent or heighten certain moods or feelings.

B. Students color the expressive portraits drawn in the previous lesson. In doing so, they select hues that they associate with the inner feelings portrayed. Students are instructed to press down firmly on the oil pastels in order to secure rich, vibrant colors. Faces *and* backgrounds are to be colored thoroughly.

C. The completed drawings of each team are exhibited in turn. As they are put on view, the remainder of the class attempts to determine the inner feelings depicted in each.

VII. EVALUATION OF THE LESSON:

A. RESPONSE:

Did students focus on the *expressive qualities* stressed by *emotionalism* when examining *de Kooning*'s painting? As a consequence, did they recognize that colors are often used in pictures to emphasize a mood or feeling?

B. PRODUCTION:

Did students use *oil pastels* to color the *expressive portraits* completed in the previous lesson? Did they make certain that the *hues* selected complemented and *emphasized* the inner feelings portrayed?

# LESSON 19–2 (Continued)

**Oil-pastel portrait (secondary-level student work)**

I. TITLE OF THE LESSON: An Abstract Wire Construction

II. DURING THIS LESSON STUDENTS ARE TO ACQUIRE INFORMATION ABOUT THE FOLLOWING:

# LESSON 19-3

| RESPONSE | | | | PRODUCTION | | | | |
|---|---|---|---|---|---|---|---|---|
| Artists or Art Objects | Period or Style | Theories of Art | Aesthetic Qualities | Subject Matter | Elements of Art | Principles of Art | Media | Techniques |
| Moore | Abstraction | | | Landscape—Abstracted | Line | Variety | Wire | Construction |
| Smith | | | | | Form | Emphasis | | |

III. OBJECTIVES:
  A. RESPONSE:
    Comparing *abstract* sculptures by *Moore* and *Smith*, students are able to distinguish the differences between them. They note that Moore's sculpture shows a concern for volume and mass, while Smith's is composed of curved and straight lines organized along a two-dimensional plane.
  B. PRODUCTION:
    Students *construct* in *wire abstract landscape* "drawings" composed of a *variety* of curved and straight *lines*. These lines are organized along a two-dimensional plane. The completed freestanding *forms* exhibit either a horizontal or a vertical *emphasis*.

IV. VISUALS:
  Moore, *Reclining Figure* (Figure 19.18)
  Smith, *Hudson River Landscape* (Figure 19.22)

V. MATERIALS AND TOOLS NEEDED FOR THIS LESSON:
  14- or 16-gauge steel wire (can be purchased at most hardware stores)
  Several pairs of side-cutting pliers (electrician's clippers) used to cut and bend wire
  Blocks of wood (not less than 10 × 10 cm [4 × 4″]) to serve as bases
  Pencils
  Newsprint
  White drawing paper (23 × 30.5 cm [9 × 12″] or larger)

VI. PRESENTATION OF THE LESSON:
  A. Students compare and contrast sculptures by Moore and Smith. Focusing on Smith's *Hudson River Landscape*, they observe how this two-dimensional design is composed of contrasting curved and straight lines. They also note that the work represents an abstraction of a landscape.
  B. Students complete several small pencil sketches of landscapes.
  C. Selecting the most successful of their landscape sketches, students reproduce them on a larger scale. They then abstract the composition by reducing it to its most essential curved and straight lines.
  D. Students are allowed the opportunity to experiment with short pieces of wire to get the feel of the material.
  E. One end of a length of wire* is fastened to a wood base. The wire is then carefully formed to make a freestanding sculpture which reproduces the abstract landscape drawing. The sculpture is composed of a variety of contrasting straight and curved lines which are organized along a two-dimensional plane.
  F. *Only one length of wire is used* to construct the sculpture. No joints will be soldered, tied, glued, or otherwise joined to each other. Support strength is to be derived from the material itself and the forms into which it is bent.

---

*Students may determine for themselves the length of this wire, although a minimum of 92 cm [36″] is usually required.

G. Monotony is avoided by varying the size and character of the shapes created with the wire line. Bends should be precise and neat. They should appear to be intentional rather than accidental.

H. The completed freestanding form must exhibit an obvious horizontal or vertical emphasis.

VII. EVALUATION OF THE LESSON:

A. RESPONSE:

Were students able to distinguish the differences between *abstract* sculptures created by *Moore* and *Smith*? Did they note the concern for volume and mass in the Moore sculpture? Were they aware of the curved and straight lines organized along a two-dimensional plane in the Smith sculpture?

B. PRODUCTION:

Did students *construct* in *wire abstract landscape* "drawings" composed of a *variety* of curved and straight *lines*? Were these lines organized along a two-dimensional plane? Did the freestanding *forms* exhibit either a horizontal or a vertical *emphasis*?

# Safety in the Art Studio

Art teachers and their students are often in daily contact with potentially harmful materials, although many may be totally unaware of it. Painters may be working with organic solvents, fiber workers with dyes and acids, and potters with glazes that contain lead, cadmium, and nickel. All these ingredients can be dangerous if not used properly. And, the list of toxic art materials does not end here. Hexane, used in rubber-cement thinner, can cause nerve damage; xylene and toluene, used in solvents and permanent magic markers, have been found to cause respiratory illnesses, genetic disorders, blood damage, and liver abnormalities; clay containing free silica and papier-mâché mixtures containing asbestos particles have been linked to silicosis and asbestosis.

Although studies have been conducted and the findings published, many teachers remain unaware that toxic substances may be in some of the art materials they use routinely in their teaching. Other teachers, aware of the problem, feel that they are exercising adequate precautions by referring to the labels on the art products they use in class. If a product falls under the category "nontoxic" as defined by the Federal Hazardous Substances Act (FHSA), these teachers feel confident that it is safe for use. They are unaware that, according to this law, the distinction between toxic and nontoxic is not as great as might be expected. This law only identifies products which are acutely toxic—those that are "near" toxic (no matter how near) may be labeled nontoxic, contributing to the belief that they are harmless.

In an effort to rectify this problem, legislation aimed at protecting users by improving the labels affixed to art products has been introduced at the federal level. Several states have also introduced or are considering similar bills. However, while progress in this regard is being made, some question the speed with which it is being made.

Not to be overlooked is the fact that the art materials industry has, for many years, supported the use of voluntary standards. These standards have been developed with the cooperation and input of various manufacturers. The Arts and Crafts Materials Institute (ACMI) has for some time adhered to a voluntary program designed to insure the safety of children working with art materials. Most art teachers are familiar with the ACMI safety labels—AP indicating Approved Product, and CP specifying Certified Product. These labels certify that the products on which they are placed have been found to contain no ingredients in sufficient quantities to be toxic or harmful to users. In addition, products with a CP seal abide by certain quality standards pertaining to workmanship, working qualities, and color.

The AP/CP seal applies to art products for younger students, while a Certified Label (CL) is intended to identify products which are appropriate for older students and adults. The CL seal on a label indicates that the product's ingredients have been examined by a toxicologist. The label lists any safety precautions required by law and by a recent labeling standard developed by the American Society of Testing and Materials.

Teachers should realize that they may also request a Material Safety Data Sheet (MSDS) from manufacturers regarding any art products they have doubts about. Among the items included on this MSDS are a listing of all the ingredients for which industrial standards exist, health hazard information, fire hazard data, and the chemicals with which the product might react dangerously.

There are certain precautions that all teachers should take into account when selecting art materials for use in their classrooms. Included in these precautions are the following:

• Make certain that the materials purchased for younger students (age 12 or under) have an AP or CP seal of approval; materials secured for use by older students should have a CL seal.

• Avoid using solvents or products containing solvents in the art room. These include turpentine, lacquer, shellac, paint thinner, rubber cement and rubber-cement thinner, permanent markers, and solvent-based inks such as silk-screen printing ink.

• Do not use acids, alkalies, or bleaches.

• Do not use aerosol spray cans since the inhalation of the spray mist can cause injury to lung tissue.

• Use dust-causing products with care in a well-ventilated area. This applies to the use of pastels, chalks, clays and plaster in dry form, copper enamels, glazes, papier-mâché mixtures, and powdered temperas.

• Place kilns in a separate room or, if that is not possible, locate the kiln in an out-of-the-way part of the room where students are not likely to come into contact with it when it is in operation. In addition, all kilns should have local exhaust ventilation.

At the beginning of each school year or new term, teachers are urged to determine if any of their students are asthmatic, visually impaired or hearing-impaired, or on prescribed medication. If asthmatic students are enrolled in the art class, they should not be exposed to dusts, fumes, or vapors because of their breathing difficulties. Visually impaired students understandably operate very close to their artwork and, as a consequence, are more likely to inhale dusts, vapors, and fumes. Students with hearing impairments should not be exposed to activities requiring loud hammering or noisy machinery. This could aggravate their condition. If students are found to be on medication, the teacher should seek a physician's advice regarding the potential harmful interaction between the prescribed medicine and art materials used in class.

Similar precautions are recommended in situations involving students who are physically handicapped, retarded, or emotionally disturbed.

The need to direct time and effort to safeguarding the health of students in the art studio cannot be ignored. Art teachers, aware of their responsibilities in this regard, recognize that assistance may be needed. Many have turned to the Center for Occupational Hazards (COH) for this assistance. COH is a national clearinghouse for research and information on health hazards in the arts. It publishes a four-page newsletter ten times a year, which covers a range of topics including new hazards, precautions, government legislation and regulations, lawsuits, and a calendar of events. Those teachers wishing to subscribe to this newsletter* or desiring additional information concerning the efforts of this not-for-profit organization can write to the following address:

The Center for Occupational Hazards
5 Beekman Street
New York, New York 10038

---

*The current subscription cost is $13 per year.

# Bibliography

## Ceramics

Ball, Carlton, and Lovoos, Janice. *Making Pottery without a Wheel: Texture and Form in Clay*. Van Nostrand Reinhold Company, New York. 1965

Kenny, John B. *The Complete Book of Pottery Making*. Chilton Book Company, New York. 1976

Krun, Josephine R. *Hand-Built Pottery*. International Textbook Company, Scranton, Pennsylvania. 1960

Nelson, Glenn C. *Ceramics*. 3rd ed. Holt, Rinehart & Winston, Inc., New York. 1983

Petterson, Henry. *Creating Form in Clay*. Van Nostrand Reinhold Company, New York. 1968

Pluckrose, Henry, ed. *Let's Model*. Van Nostrand Reinhold Company, New York. 1971

Pucci, Cora. *Pottery: A Basic Manual*. Little, Brown & Company, Boston. 1974

Roettger, Ernst. *Creative Clay Design*. Van Nostrand Reinhold Company, New York. 1972

Sanders, Herbert H. *Sunset Ceramics Book*. Lane Magazine and Book Company, Menlo Park, California. 1953

Sellers, Thomas, ed. *Ceramic Projects*. Professional Publications, Inc., Columbus, Ohio. 1981

Villard, Paul. *A First Book of Ceramics*. Funk & Wagnalls Company, New York. 1969

## Crafts

Argiro, Larry. *Mosaic Art Today*. International Textbook Company, Scranton, Pennsylvania. 1961

Bovin, Murray. *Jewelry Making for Schools, Tradesmen, Craftsmen*. Murray Brown Publisher, Forest Hills, New Jersey. 1979

Conway, Vallery. *Introducing Enameling*. Watson-Guptill Publications, New York. 1973

Gentile, Thomas. *Step-by-Step Jewelry*. Golden Press, New York. 1968

Horn, George. *Crafts for Today's Schools*. Davis Publications, Inc., Worcester, Massachusetts. 1972

Laliberte, Norman, and McIlhany, Sterling. *Banners and Hangings*. Van Nostrand Reinhold Company, New York. 1966

Maile, Anne. *Tie and Dye as Present-Day Craft*. Taplinger Publishing Company, Inc., New York. 1971

Marthann, Alexander. *Simple Weaving*. Taplinger Publishing Company, Inc., New York. 1969

Phillips, May Walker. *Step-by-Step Macramé*. Golden Press, New York. 1970

Plath, Iona. *Handweaving*. Charles Scribner's Sons, New York. 1964

Rainey, Sarita. *Weaving without a Loom*. Davis Publications, Inc., Worcester, Massachusetts. 1983

Rose, Grace B. *Illustrated Encyclopedia of Crafts and How to Make Them*. Doubleday & Company, Inc., New York. 1978

Short, E. *Introducing Macramé*. Watson-Guptill Publications, New York. 1973

Znamierowski, Nell. *Step-by-Step Weaving*. Golden Press, New York. 1967

## Drawing

Albert, C., and Seckler, D. *Figure Drawing Comes to Life*. Van Nostrand Reinhold Company, New York. 1957

Brommer, Gerald F. *Drawing* (revised edition). Davis Publications, Inc., Worcester, Massachusetts. 1978

Calle, Paul. *The Pencil*. Watson-Guptill Publications, New York. 1975

Chaet, Bernard. *The Art of Drawing*. Holt, Rinehart & Winston, Inc., New York. 1978

Edwards, Betty. *Drawing on the Right Side of the Brain*. Houghton Mifflin Company, Boston, Massachusetts. 1979

Greene, Daniel. *Pastel: A Comprehensive Guide to Pastel Painting*. Watson-Guptill Publications, New York. 1974

James, Jane H. *Perspective Drawing*. Prentice-Hall, Englewood Cliffs, New Jersey. 1981

Kaupelis, Robert. *Learning to Draw*. Watson-Guptill Publications, New York. 1983

Pitz, Henry C. *Ink Drawing Techniques*. Watson-Guptill Publications, New York. 1957

Porter, Albert. *The Art of Sketching*. Davis Publications, Inc., Worcester, Massachusetts. 1977

Purser, Stuart. *The Drawing Handbook*. Davis Publications, Inc. Worcester, Massachusetts. 1976

Rawson, Philip. *The Art of Drawing*. Prentice-Hall, Englewood Cliffs, New Jersey. 1984

Thompson, Beatrice. *Drawings by High School Students*. Reinhold Publishing Corporation, New York. 1966

Weiss, Harvey. *Pencil, Pen and Brush*. Scholastic Inc., New York. 1974

Winter, Roger. *Introduction to Drawing*. Prentice-Hall, Englewood Cliffs, New Jersey. 1983

## Painting

Brommer, Gerald F. *Transparent Watercolor: Ideas and Techniques*. Davis Publications, Inc., Worcester, Massachusetts. 1973

Chomicky, Yar. *Watercolor Painting*. Prentice-Hall, Inc., Englewood Cliffs, New Jersey. 1968

Davidson, Morris. *Painting with a Purpose*. Prentice-Hall, Inc., Englewood Cliffs, New Jersey. 1969

Laidman, Hugh. *The Complete Book of Drawing and Painting*. The Viking Press, New York. 1974

Mayer, Ralph. *The Painter's Craft*. Penguin Books, Inc., New York. 1979

Sheaks, Barclay. *Painting with Acrylics: From Start to Finish*. Davis Publications, Inc., Worcester, Massachusetts. 1972

Timmons, Virginia. *Painting: Ideas, Materials, Processes*. Davis Publications, Inc., Worcester, Massachusetts. 1978

Woody, Russell. *Painting with Synthetic Media*. Van Nostrand Reinhold Company, New York. 1964

## Photography

Cooke, Robert W. *Designing with Light on Paper and Film*. Davis Publications, Inc., Worcester, Massachusetts. 1969

Davis, Phil. *Photography*. 2nd ed. William C. Brown Co., Dubuque, Iowa. 1982

Eastman Kodak. *Movies and Slides without a Camera*. Rochester, New York. 1972

Holter, Patra. *Photography without a Camera*. Van Nostrand Reinhold Company, New York. 1980

Horvath, Joan. *Film Making for Beginners*. Thomas Nelson, Inc., New York. 1977

Rhode, Robert B., and McCall, Floyd. *Introduction to Photography*. 4th ed. Macmillan Publishing Co., New York. 1981

Simon, Michael, and Moore, Dennis. *First Lessons in Black and White Photography*. Holt, Rinehart & Winston, Inc., New York. 1978

## Printmaking

Andrews, Michael F. *Creative Printmaking*. Prentice-Hall, Englewood Cliffs, New Jersey. 1963

Biegeleisen, J.I. *Screen Printing*. Watson-Guptill Publications, New York. 1971

Brommer, Gerald F. *Relief Printmaking*. Davis Publications, Inc., Worcester, Massachusetts. 1970

Capon, Robin. *Introducing Abstract Printmaking*. Watson-Guptill Publications, New York. 1974

Erickson, Jane, and Sproul, Adelaide. *Printmaking without a Press*. Reinhold Publishing Corporation, New York. 1966

Gorbaty, Norman. *Printmaking with a Spoon*. Van Nostrand Reinhold Company. 1960

McArthur, Jeanette. *Printing without a Press*. Dukane Press, Inc., Hollywood, California. 1970

Ross, John, and Romano, Clare. *The Complete New Techniques in Printmaking*. Free Press, New York. 1974

Ross, John, and Romano, Clare. *The Complete Screen Print and Lithograph*. Free Press, New York. 1974

Weiss, Harvey. *Paper, Ink and Roller*. William R. Scott, Inc., New York. 1958

Zaidenberg, Arthur. *Prints and How to Make Them*. Harper & Row, Publishers, New York. 1964

## Sculpture

Averback, Arnold. *Modelled Sculpture and Plaster Casting*. Thomas Yoseloff, New York. 1961

Baldwin, John. *Contemporary Sculpture Techniques*. Reinhold Publishing Corporation, New York. 1967

Brommer, Gerald F. *Wire Sculpture and Other Three Dimensional Construction*. Davis Publications, Inc., Worcester, Massachusetts. 1968

Clarke, Geoffrey, and Stroud, Cornock. *A Sculptor's Manual*. Reinhold Book Corporation, New York. 1968

Eliscu, Frank. *Sculpture Techniques in Clay, Wax, and Slate*. Arts and Crafts Book Club, Great Neck, New York. 1961

Helfman, Harry. *Making Your Own Sculpture*. William Morrow & Co., Inc., New York. 1971

Lanten, Edouard. *Modelling and Sculpture*. Dover Publications, New York. 1965

Marks, Mickey. *Sand Sculpture*. The Dial Press, New York. 1963

Meilach, Dona Z., and Meilach, Melvin. *Box Art: Assemblage and Construction*. Crown Publishers, Inc., New York. 1975

Meilach, Dona Z. *Soft Sculpture and Other Soft Art Forms*. Crown Publishers, Inc., New York. 1974

Reed, Carl, and Orze, Joseph. *Art from Scrap*. Davis Publications, Inc., Worcester, Massachusetts. 1973

Reed, Carl, and Towne, Burt. *Sculpture from Found Objects*. Davis Publications, Inc., Worcester, Massachusetts. 1974

Sadler, Arthur. *Paper Sculpture*. Blanford Press, Ltd., London. 1955

Stribling, Mary Lou. *Art from Found Materials*. Crown Publishers, Inc., New York. 1971

Struppeck, Jules. *The Creation of Sculpture*. Holt, Rinehart & Winston, New York. 1952

Verhilst, Wilbart. *Sculpture: Tools, Materials and Techniques*. Prentice-Hall, Englewood Cliffs, New Jersey. 1973

Wittkower, Rudolph. *Sculpture: Processes and Principles*. Allen Lane, London. 1977

# Art Resources: Slides, Films, and Reproductions

Art is a visual medium and certainly no one is more conscious of this than art teachers. A great many of these teachers make frequent use of slides and other visual aids to enrich their instruction in criticism, history, and studio. And, as a consequence, they are always on the alert for new sources of slides, films, and reproductions.

## Art Slides

Most art teachers discover early in their careers that museums and galleries often allow visitors to take photographs and slides of the artworks on display. It is not surprising then that the 35-mm camera is one of the art teacher's most valued instructional tools. It is put to continual use in taking slides of local artworks (including student work) as well as artworks encountered during extended trips. And, teachers have discovered that students seem to exhibit greater interest and become more actively involved in lessons in which the teacher presents for discussion slides he or she has taken personally. In such instances, students recognize that the teacher's comments are based upon actual contact with original works of art, and this contributes to the student's curiosity. This curiosity is often reflected in increased attention and a greater volume of questions pertaining to the artworks. After all, they reason, the teacher has been there and actually viewed "the real thing." It follows then that the teacher is in a position to answer questions, provide pertinent facts, and express personal impressions.

Teachers have also discovered that most museums and galleries sell slides of the artworks in their collections. Practically every museum in the country has a museum shop where slides of the major works in the collection can be purchased. The same can be said for museums, galleries, and important artistic sites in other countries. However, the quality of these slides varies almost as much as does the price.

To be certain of good-quality art slides at a modest price, many teachers have elected to begin their collections by purchasing slides from the National Gallery of Art in Washington, D.C. Drawing on this highly recommended source, it is possible for the teacher to assemble not only slides but various types of color reproductions of artworks in the Gallery. Hundreds of subjects are available in slides made individually from the paintings and sculptures comprising the Gallery's extensive collection. Most of these works are also reproduced in relatively inexpensive 28 × 36-cm [11 × 14-inch] color prints as well as larger reproductions. Discounts on these and many other items are available to educational institutions on orders over a certain nominal amount. For further information, teachers are advised to contact the Publications Service of the National Gallery of Art, Washington D.C. 20565. At the same time, they should request the current *Catalog of Reproductions and Publications*, which contains a listing and prices for color slides, books, catalogs, and other educational materials.

Of course, teachers should also make a point of contacting nearby museums and galleries to determine if they provide similar resources for educators. A visit to these institutions could pay large dividends in the form of slide-tape presentations, color reproductions, and books. And, the contact may be the first step in scheduling class tours or arranging for workshops and special lectures.

*It is impossible to exaggerate the importance of museum visitations by students.* These visitations enable students to view and study original works of art rather than projected slide images or other reproductions. The conditions of a museum visit are very different from those in which students view slides of paintings and other artworks in class. For one thing, the projected image in the classroom distorts the size, shape, and color of original paintings. The problem is magnified when slides of sculpture and other three-dimensional art forms are studied. These slides present the art object from a fixed vantage point and in a particular light and prohibit the student from observing and responding to the subtleties and intricacies of form, texture, and value inherent in three-dimensional art forms.

To take maximum advantage of museum visits, teachers should prepare their students beforehand and reinforce the visitation with a follow-up program upon returning to the classroom. References to sections in *Art in Focus* pertaining to specific artists, artworks, or artistic styles represented in the museum collections should aid those efforts. In addition, several of the Criticism and History Experiences given for each chapter of *Art in Focus* and found at the end of the text describe learning experiences that could be even more effective if tied to museum visitations. These activities and variations on them could be presented in class before and after museum visits.

A comprehensive listing of art-slide suppliers from all over the world can be found in a publication known as the *Slide Buyer's Guide*. The most recent edition of this *Guide*, published by the Visual Resources Association and Libraries Unlimited, can be purchased for a nominal price by contacting Libraries Unlimited, P.O. Box 263, Littleton, Colorado 80106.

As an immediate aid to teachers, the following select list of slide sources in the United States is provided. Requests for catalogs and slide lists from these sources should be made on school stationery in order to take advantage of discounts frequently provided to educational institutions.

## Museum and Gallery Sources

Albright-Knox Art Gallery
1285 Elmwood Avenue
Buffalo, New York 14222

An emphasis is placed on modern painting and sculpture in this good-quality slide collection.

Amon Carter Museum of Western Art
3501 Camp Bowie Boulevard
Fort Worth, Texas 76107

Slides of artworks by artists associated with the frontier West of the late 19th century. Slides are of excellent quality.

Dayton Art Institute
Forest and Riverview Avenue
Dayton, Ohio 45401

A list of good-quality slides of works in the collection is available on request.

Detroit Institute of Arts
Slide Order Department
5200 Woodward Avenue
Detroit, Michigan 48202

Color is generally good in this extensive collection of art slides.

Kimbell Art Museum
Will Rogers Road West
Fort Worth, Texas 76107

Slides of European art from Classical times to the early 20th century are available. A list of these good-quality slides is available.

Los Angeles County Art Museum
5905 Wilshire Boulevard
Los Angeles, California 90036

Good-quality slides are available individually or in sets of slides, five slides per set.

Metropolitan Museum of Art
255 Gracie Station
New York, New York 10028

The slides available are of good quality; some sets are excellent. Included in these are sets entitled "The Year 1200" and "The Unicorn Tapestries."

Milwaukee Art Center
750 North Lincoln Memorial Drive
Milwaukee, Wisconsin 53202

Will provide a list of slides from their permanent collection as well as a list of instructional packages. The quality of the slides is good.

Minneapolis Institute of Arts
2400 3rd Avenue South
Minneapolis, Minnesota 55404

Provides good-quality slides with discounts available for quantity purchases.

Museum of Fine Arts
465 Huntington Avenue
Boston, Massachusetts 02115

Offers a good selection of slide sets ranging from ten to eighty slides per set. Good quality noted in the slides available.

Museum of Fine Arts
1001 Bissonet Street
Houston, Texas 77005

Provides slides of good quality.

Museum of Modern Art
11 West 53rd Street
New York, New York 10019

Educational discounts available on slides in their extensive collection. Quality is good.

National Gallery of Art
Publications Service
6th and Constitution Avenue
Washington, D.C. 20565

Provides a catalog of their extensive collection of excellent art slides.

North Carolina Museum of Art
107 E. Morgan Street
Raleigh, North Carolina 27601

Phillips Collection
1600 21st Street, N.W.
Washington, D.C. 20009

Philadelphia Museum of Art
Parkway at 26th Street
Philadelphia, Pennsylvania 19102

St. Louis Art Museum
Forest Park
St. Louis, Missouri 63110

Solomon R. Guggenheim Museum
1071 Fifth Avenue
New York, New York 10028

Whitney Museum of American Art
945 Madison Avenue
New York, New York 10021

An extensive slide collection. Be certain to ask about the many excellent services provided to educators by this museum.

An extensive slide collection with discounts available on quantity purchases. Quality is good.

Catalogs of slide holdings are available at a nominal price. Individual catalogs on painting; architecture; sculpture; manuscripts and prints; costumes, rugs, tapestries, and textiles. Slide collection covers works in the museum as well as works from other sources. Encompasses the entire range of art history. Slides are of good quality.

Address an inquiry to the Teachers Resource Center to secure a catalog of over 3,000 good-quality art slides at a nominal price.

The slides available from this collection are excellent in terms of color and detail.

Good-quality slides of American painting and sculpture.

## Commercial Suppliers

Color Slide Enterprises
Box 150
Oxford, Ohio 45056

I.W. Protheroe: Fine Arts Slides
P.O. Box 898
Chula Vista, California 92102

Prothmann Associates, Inc.
650 Thomas Avenue
Baldwin, New York 11510

Rosenthal Art Slides
5456 South Ridgewood Court
Chicago, Illinois 60615

Sandak, Inc.
180 Harvard Avenue
Stamford, Connecticut 06902

University Prints
21 East Street
Winchester, Massachusetts 01890

American Library Color Slide Co., Inc.
P.O. Box 5810
Grand Central Station
New York, New York 10017

Many slides available from the sources listed here as well as those specified in the *Slide Buyer's Guide* can be obtained in either cardboard or glass mounts. Cardboard mounts are, of course, less expensive, but glass mounts protect the film against damage caused by dust and fingerprints. Inexpensive slides are usually duplicates in that they are not made from original film. Instead, they are re-photographed from the

original film. As a result, some loss of detail can be expected, although this loss is not usually apparent except to a specialist familiar with the photographed work.

Over time, slides will deteriorate because chemical changes within the dyes cause the colors to yellow. The type of film, the mounting, and the care given to slides will determine their life expectancy. As a general rule, good-quality slides will last from three to ten or more years. To assure maximum life for their slides, teachers should store them away from direct sunlight and avoid touching the film. An effective way of storing a collection of slides is in loose-leaf notebooks. Transparent plastic slide sheets holding twenty slides can be purchased in any photo store and placed within these notebooks. Slides can then be inserted and filed according to period, style, artist, subject matter, medium, etc. To select a slide, the teacher merely extracts the plastic sheet from the notebook and holds it up to the light.

## Art Films and Reproductions

The following selection of sources for art films and reproductions has been compiled as a further aid to teachers seeking instructional materials.

### Sources for Art Films
ACI Films, Inc.
16 West 46th Street
New York, New York 10036

Bailey Film Associated
11559 Santa Monica Boulevard
Los Angeles, California 90025

Brandon Films, Inc.
244 Kearney Street
San Francisco, California 94108

Coronet Instructional Films
65 E. South Water Street
Coronet Building
Chicago, Illinois 60610

Canadian Centre for Films on Art
P.O. Box/CP 457
Ottawa 2, Ontario, Canada

Columbia University Center for Mass Communication
West 113th Street
New York, New York 10025

Carson Davidson
86 Bedford Street
New York, New York 10014

Churchill Films
662 North Robertson Boulevard
Los Angeles, California 90096

Gotham Films Production
11 East 44th Street
New York, New York 10017

Encyclopedia Britannica Films
425 Michigan Avenue
Chicago, Illinois 60611

Educational Audio Visual, Inc.
Pleasantville, New York 10570

International Film Bureau
332 S. Michigan Avenue
Chicago, Illinois 60604

Hester and Associates
11422 Harry Hines Boulevard
Dallas, Texas 75229

Janus Films
745 Fifth Avenue
New York, New York 10022

McGraw-Hill Textfilms
1221 Avenue of the Americas
New York, New York 10020

Museum at Large, Ltd., Films
157 West 54th Street
New York, New York 10019

Museum of Modern Art
11 West 53rd Street
New York, New York 10019

National Film Board of Canada
400 West Madison Street
Chicago, Illinois 60606

Peckham Productions
c/o National Gallery of Art
Washington, D.C. 20565

Pyramid Films
P.O. Box 1048
Santa Monica, California 90404

Radim Films, Inc.
17 West 60th Street
New York, New York 10023

Time-Life Films
43 West 16th Street
New York, New York 10011

United World Films
221 Park Avenue South
New York, New York 10003

Warren Schloat Productions, Inc.
Pleasantville, New York 10570

## Sources for Art Reproductions

Harry N. Abrams
110 East 59th Street
New York, New York 10022

Artext Prints, Inc.
Westport, Connecticut 06880

Metropolitan Museum of Art
Fifth Avenue and 82nd Street
New York, New York 10028

Museum of Modern Art
11 West 53rd Street
New York, New York 10019

National Gallery of Art
Publications Service
6th and Constitution Avenue
Washington, D.C. 20565

New York Graphic Society
140 Greenwich Avenue
Greenwich, Connecticut 06830

North Carolina Museum of Art
Education Services
107 E. Morgan Street
Raleigh, North Carolina 27601

Oestreicher's Prints, Inc.
43 West 46th Street
New York, New York 10036

Penn Print Company
572 Fifth Avenue
New York, New York 10036

Dr. Konrad Prothmann
2378 Soper Avenue
Baldwin, New York 11510

Shorewood Reproductions, Inc.
Department 2
724 Fifth Avenue
New York, New York 10019

University Prints
21 East Street
Winchester, Massachusetts 01890

# Handout Materials